MY LOVE MY ENEMY

MY LOVE MY ENEMY

MEDITATIONS FOR THE SEPARATED

PAT MORGAN

NORTHFIELD PUBLISHING
CHICAGO

Northfield Publishing
A Division of MBI
Chicago, IL

ISBN: 1-881273-03-2

1 3 5 7 9 10 8 6 4 2

Printed in the United States of America

This book is dedicated to my children and
to all of the family, friends, co-workers, and teachers
who shared with me of themselves over my lifetime.
God used the resources of their experience, love, and faith
to prepare me to survive this great crisis in my life.

Contents

Acknowledgments

Since this book is written under a pen name, my acknowledgments must also follow the same format. Thanks to the Mongoose who would not let this die and helped with editing. Duncan, Anne, Ella, and others at Northfield Publishing have smoothed some rough spots and have made valuable improvements. Pierre kept my poor old computer going. My appreciation also goes to the gang of eight and other friends who laughed and cried through this manuscript while making valuable suggestions. My dog also insisted on a credit, or she threatened to sue.

Preface

I have been separated from my wife for the past year. She left and my world collapsed. What I have written here is part of the kaleidoscope of feelings and thoughts that have been a part of this time of separation.

There are many books available on "How to Have a Happy Marriage" or "Now That You Are Divorced . . . ," but I found little to help me during the time of separation. It is a horrible purgatory when reconciliation or divorce are both still possible. How do you cope with that uncertainty in such a crucial area of life?

This book is raw in its emotions because that is how it feels to face this kind of crisis. For those who must face a marriage breakdown, I hope this book will give the comfort of shared experience. For those who as friends, family, or in ministry are dealing with people in crisis, perhaps this book will be a glimpse into one experience of this kind of pain.

The mix of humor and pain in this book is real for me. It does not make light of the anguish but is very much a part of the process in my experience. Call it gallows humor or just a part of surviving.

Out of respect for my wife, I am using a pen name in this book and assumed names for her and others. What I can tell you is that I had the benefit of growing up in a good religious home. I was active in my church and attended a fine nondenominational college. My wife, who had a similar upbringing, and I met at camp and dated for three years before our marriage. We pastored a small country church for a few years and then became "tent makers"—going into business so that we had income coming in at the same time we served our denomination and started a church.

I love my wife, and, despite our problems, I would still have married her if I had known then what I know now. We have two beautiful preschool children, who along with my wife were the joy of my life in this world.

This is not a book about who's "at fault." All marriages are a collection of two people's strengths, weaknesses, histories, choices, hopes, dreams, and failures. I do not believe that the notion of an "innocent party" is either helpful or honest since we are all far too experienced sinners saved by grace. I hope that you sense that this is not a book of answers or magic wands (if you do have any extra wands, please contact the publisher!).

I pray that this book might help you or a loved one through a tough time, if that is what awaits.

1

In a Very Small Room—Surrounded by Porcupines

Being alone again after a decade of marriage brings with it a strange mix of feelings. I would have thought that with the loneliness would come a great sense of freedom to do what I wanted when I wanted. My time would be my own. There would be no one to consult about plans for an evening or a day off.

To my surprise, this aloneness is claustrophobic. Everything I do hurts. When I am at home, I am smothered by reminders of her. Unpacking boxes is a never-ending task because every box contains some special pain.

Some, like her wedding dress, are obvious. Others, like a scribbled note to another Sunday school worker, stabs with surprising force. It is just a simple note to a teacher a year ago about a lesson plan long since taught. But it is in her writing. It has her name at the bottom of the tiny page.

I had never realized how many memories attach themselves to each piece of trinket or trash. Each represents a moment in time when things were different—when we were husband and wife, when we were a family.

What was happening in our life when we bought that Christmas globe with the snowman inside that played "Frosty the Snow Man" over and over again? That's right, we were expecting our firstborn.

I remember picking out the dishes before we were married. We were in a store with a very long row of fine china of all colors and designs. I said to my love, "Let's each look them over and see which one we would choose." With all those choices, we both chose the same pattern. What fun! But now, those dishes seem to be sad too. So much has changed. Everything I do hurts.

Others say how well I am doing. They don't know how small this house has become. They don't know that wherever I turn, a porcupine waits with quills pointed at me. I can't stand still, but it hurts to move. Home used to be such a safe place. I was comforted by happy reminders of special memories. All of those warm fuzzies now sting and cut me. I am in a very small room—surrounded by porcupines.

2

When the Cavalry Doesn't Come over the Hill

I used to love watching westerns as a kid. It was easy to tell the good guys from the bad—white hats and black. The good guys would get into awful situations, but you knew deep down that just before they were to be killed the cavalry would come over the hill. You could allow yourself to be really scared because you knew there would be a happy ending for the hero.

This is a really scary time. I never liked a disaster movie or a retelling of the Alamo. Sure, there were the heroics of facing the bitter end bravely, but bitter ends are just that. No, I preferred the cavalry charge being heard over the next ridge and seeing the bad guys wince in anticipation.

With "Anne" gone saying that she is never coming back, I must face the fact that in my "movie" I may be the one at the Little Big Horn. God may not send help in time to rescue my marriage. Marriages—even Christian marriages—do not always have happy endings. I always imagined growing old together, holding hands as we rocked together on the front porch in our nineties telling jokes and reminiscing about an interesting life. Separation and "the D word" were always out of the question. Now she is gone and so is the rocking chair.

How do I make sense out of the news that the cavalry is busy somewhere else? I have experienced the grace of God in my life. I know His power to draw me to Himself in love. I have experienced His Spirit's conviction when I have wandered away. So has Anne. Why can't the God of peace help us out of our crisis now? Where is grace? Why won't He send help to us? If not for our sake, for the sake of the children's well-being?

I listen for the sound of distant horses. I long for that trumpet so that I can start breathing again. I want to find a mirror and look in it. Whose face will I see? Roy Rogers? Or General George Custer? I want the chance for us to have happy trails again. But I fear there will be blood everywhere and that this scalp will be hanging on Satan's spear as a trophy.

Telegram to the Commander in Chief:

URGENT . . . STOP . . . GOD, PLEASE HURRY . . . STOP . . . RUNNING OUT OF AMMUNITION AND SUPPLIES . . . STOP . . . ENEMY HAS US SURROUNDED . . . STOP . . . CAN'T HOLD OUT MUCH LONGER . . . STOP . . . FEAR MASSACRE OF MARRIAGE . . . STOP . . . PLEASE SEND CAVALRY . . .

3

The Sounds of Silence

O *God, I am so alone.* All around me it is quiet. Not the quiet of a gentle meadow in summer but the eerie silence of a tomb. I am glad for the ticking clock. The sound of a passing car brings relief. Somewhere, something is alive.

Some squirrels have found their way into the attic. I hear their scratching over my bedroom ceiling. I try to picture them up there. Gray squirrels, I think. But then I see them together as a family. Things must be tough—I am jealous of the squirrels.

I do not hear her singing anymore. Oh, she wasn't the type to always go around singing, but I do remember her singing. Once she was happy. Now she is gone. Is she singing at her apartment? I miss the sound of her voice. It was gentle but clear. Anne always reminded me of Karen Carpenter. She is gone, too.

Hearing Anne talk was special. I can still imagine the sentences she would form. It's like Mr. Spock's creating the captain's voice on the computer on "Star Trek." I imagine hearing Anne speak again to me with kindness and love. But then silence invades and stops the voice.

Where is the sound of my children? Their laughter and tears and their joy of life fill my soul. But today they are just echoes of other times. They are coming again next Thursday. I can hang on another week. I miss you, Jeff and Laura. It is so quiet. So many hours with so few sounds.

I can remember times at home when I went to the study for some quiet. It is a strange thought now. Now I try to think about where I can go for some noise! Many evenings, just to be around people I have gone to sit in the stands at a local baseball or hockey field to watch teenagers play. I can see why nightclubs and bars are favorite places for singles and singles again. You can drown out the silence.

Worst of all is God's silence. Oh, I know about Schaeffer's book telling us that "He is there, and He is not silent." But He isn't saying anything to me right now. It feels like a very big, cold shoulder.

I can imagine someone else praying for me right now. "God in heaven, I want to pray for Pat. He is really struggling . . ." Then God interrupts. "Who?" The friend answers, "Morgan—Pat Morgan. He was our pastor once and his wife left—You know?" God might then say, "Pat Morgan? . . . No, I can't say that I ever heard of him . . ."

Maybe it is the child in all of us that needs God's reassurance. We need to be held and comforted by God. I remember when I felt so close to Him. What is different now? God doesn't move. *Are You there, God?* Only sounds of silence answer.

4

When Friends Throw You Anchors

My universe has shrunk quickly. As though it had been swallowed in a black hole, all light in my life has disappeared, and so much of what was my life is now gone. Where are all my friends—points of light in my night's sky?

Some are still there. Thank God for them. But some of the people who were so important a few months ago have not only gone but have hit me with some parting shots.

Like a drowning swimmer, I need a life preserver. Some friends throw them to me. A couple overthrow by giving me all of the quick answers about how God is working all of this out for my good. Others underthrow with a simple "I'll pray for you" followed by definite withdrawal. Others miss the mark. "She isn't coming back—get on with your life," or, "If you have faith, God will bring her back."

As a lifeguard, I was taught the rules: "Reach, throw, row, tow, and go." That was the sequence of rescue to be followed when someone was drowning. The last thing that you do is to make contact, since the drowning victim might drag you down, too. Good advice for lifeguarding but a tough way to help someone who is separated.

The key for the rescuer is to keep talking to the drowning victim. He must be reassured that he is going to make it. It is hearing that strong voice that helps the person at risk to begin to trust. Without trust, there can be no rescue. The lifeguard knows that ultimately the swimmer must make a decision to trust him. Then begins the long swim back.

But some friends cannot cope with your distress. Some actually look to you for comfort. They want reassurance that this could not happen to them, too.

The most painful rescuer to cope with is the friend who has been waiting for a long time to tell you all that is wrong with you. Since your spouse now agrees that things are bad enough to leave, he calls with his list of points of fault that you have had and expresses surprise that your spouse stayed as long as she did. Seeking to understand what went wrong and feeling like a failure, you encourage him to keep talking. As he rips away at you, you ask whether these are problems your wife has mentioned. “Oh, I would never break a confidence with her.” It is a heavy anchor to catch while you are busy drowning.

5

Honest to God

I might have titled this chapter "Cursing God—And Not Dying—More Foul Luck," but "Honest to God" is probably apt, too. I hope that what I write here does not disturb you too much. But I suspect that if you are sharing this or another excruciating pain, you will know what I am saying.

We all are weaker in some areas of life and stronger in others. One of the stronger areas of self-control for me was language. I did not swear, curse, or use vulgarities. For whatever reason, that was not a serious area of temptation for me. It was just the way I was, as a rule. Perhaps it was my awareness of the power of words to heal or to harm that helped me in this area.

Well, since my wife left, my dog could mistake me for General Patton. It is a strange phenomenon. I am walking around the house—and find myself swearing. At times, my swearing is prompted by looking at her picture. At other times it is prompted by a commercial portraying a happy family or couple. Or I might swear for no reason at all. The anger that her rejection of me engendered—added to my guilt and compounded by my sense of hopelessness—does some strange things.

At times I seem to step outside of myself and watch myself cursing and swearing. Blind rage overwhelms and controls me. Like a victim of Gilles de la Tourette's Syndrome, the disorder that makes its victims curse and insult others uncontrollably, I do not recognize myself. I just spew out like a volcano with hot lava words and phrases that scorch the air.

My anger then turns to God. My faith, theology, and experience tell me that God can intervene in our lives. I have experienced His correction and encouragement before. So had Anne. With clenched fists and face I shout my curses at God for ignoring us in our time of need. *You could do something about this! I hate You for putting us all* (and especially me?) *through this pain. What do You want, God? Do You want me to quit? Do You want me to abandon my faith? Do You want me to promise that I will never be involved in ministry again? Do You want to see me break—pushing and pushing until I go over the edge? You are such a sadistic God. What do You want from me? I want to see if my birth certificate was wrong—is my name really Esau?*

Even as I write those words, I want to fill this page with "expletives not deleted." I have had some pretty convincing hate sessions with God. When God watches me explode like this, is He filled with the same mix of feelings I experience as a parent when I watch our two year old, Laura, throw a tantrum? I feel the rage and frustration of the child. I know that she has lost perspective and is acting out in the only way she knows how. I reach out to hug her in her pain, to reassure her of my love, knowing that her yelling and screaming will not solve her dilemma.

I have a very high view of the sovereign position of God. I do not take lightly His power or majesty. My reverence for God is profound. But perhaps I take courage from my knowledge of the biblical characters. Many of them—especially

David and some of the minor prophets—were painfully transparent with God. Maybe it is my conviction that God is love that allows me to express my pain and frustration with Him. In a strange way, I am secure enough in my relationship with Christ to let my pain speak unedited. I know that He understands my fear and my hurt.

The essence of being left by a spouse is rejection. Jesus experienced the rejection of the world He came to save when He hung on a cross. He even experienced God's rejection as He bore the sins of the world. There is healing in my transparency with God. I know that His love for me is unconditional. That gives me the courage to be honest to God.

6

Vows of Silence

One of the basic characteristics of my relationship with my wife was my respect for her. I think that I would have received an A+ for honoring. A big part of that was that I was very careful to never speak critically of her to anyone else. That practice was not a pretense that she was or we were perfect, but rather it was part of a basic commitment to demonstrate my love for her by not criticizing her in front of others. When we disagreed or I was unhappy about something, we confronted the issues privately. Call it vows of silence.

Watching other husbands make their wives the butt of jokes or put them down as people was hard for me to tolerate. Didn't they see the look of pain on their spouse's face? Didn't they know what it said about them if their spouse really was "stupid" or an "airhead"?

I guess that I would make a good Republican, since their eleventh commandment is "Thou shalt not speak ill of a fellow Republican." It was important to me to always speak well of my love and praise her to other people.

Now I find myself in a process that forces me to tell counselors, social workers, lawyers, and courts about Anne's negative traits and actions. That has been one of the worst aspects of this experience. I wish I had put it on a videotape the first time and then said to all of the subsequent professionals, "I don't want to have to get into this with you—here is my life and wife's story on VCR."

Worse yet, I am in a position where my wife must be confronted with her past and problems. I have found this so difficult that the emotions and pain have led me to do and say things that compound the problem. I soon realized that I would not be perfect in handling the matter, and so have settled for a great batting average of .400 rather than a gymnast's goal of a perfect 10.0.

It happened first the night she walked out. She drove off without warning and stayed with another couple. She made clear that she was not coming back that night, and I sensed that she was really going for good.

It was ironic that as the Berlin Wall was falling in Germany, Anne was erecting a wall between us. Crossing the line she had created would risk an exchange of gunfire. No truce or white flag was allowed by Anne from the beginning. All I could see was more and more machine gun turrets being erected by her. All I could do was write my graffiti of pain on my side of the wall. Graffiti she never read.

Our first experience in court over the children represented a limited nuclear exchange. I am sure that she saw the court process as threatening and offensive. She used the occasion to say in her affidavit all of the things about my past that would be harmful to me. It hurt to read that document. It hurt to know that on the public record was a list of my sins and past failures. It hurt that none of them had any relevance to the children's issues, the reason we were there.

As the custody problems drag on, the prospects are that a judge will order psychiatric assessments of each of us to determine what arrangement will be in the best interests of the children. I do not look forward to yet another person's learning my view of my wife's problems as they affect the children. I hate it.

How do I handle the overt and implied questions in peoples' words and eyes? I want to help, not diagnose. I don't want to hurt her. *Lord, I don't want to break my vows of silence.*

7

Your Dog as Analyst

My poor dog. It is a wonder that she did not run away, too. After nine years of friendly people being around and more recently a couple of enthusiastic children, now she has to put up with a deranged master. She would not have recommended a dog's life to you at my house.

In the beginning of the separation, Toffee howled incessantly. I appreciated her empathy, if not the noise. She moped around looking forlorn. Looking out the window by the children's play table, she watched the road for some sign that her mistress and children would come back. It was a lonely vigil.

With no one else to talk with, I hired my dog as my off-hours counselor. I sat by the fireplace in our bedroom and talked to the dog for hours on end. That might suggest I could become prime minister of Canada, as I understand that one of their longest-serving leaders, Mackenzie King, used to talk with his dog at length (although I believe that his dog was already dead—but I digress). I suspect that the dog went to a school where the Carl Rogers's nondirective method of counseling was taught. In the face of all my questions, comments, and observations, that dog was able to avoid giving me any answers. I am sure that her professors would have been proud of her self-discipline. There were times when I thought she was going to say something. Then she would lower her head and sigh. I think we called them "eloquent grunts" in communications class.

She did have ways of effective nonverbal communication that were unmistakable. When we left the matrimonial home to move up to a rental house in the town where my wife had moved with the children, the dog became very explicit. I could regularly count on her having intentional accidents in the house no matter how often she went outside. I have an excellent gag reflex that works very well any time a clean-up is required. On more than one occasion, I have had to remove my mess as well as hers.

On one weekend when the children were with me the dog made three "statements." The first was in front of our now five-year-old son, Jeff, who was standing by the open door, coaxing her to leave. A couple of hours later, Toffee repeated the performance. Overnight she made her third deposit by the door. Jeff woke me up with the news. I picked up the small mat with the deposit on it and set it outside the door to be cleaned after our morning showers. I had no sooner finished my shower and dressed then there came a knock on the door. A young aggressive salesman had arrived to sell encyclopedias. After three firm nos, he realized that there would be no sale today. He turned and walked away. As I looked at his shoes, I smiled with the realization that the salesman had at least taken a "deposit" with him.

Yes, my dog has influenced many people over the years. If she only knew how close she has come to a permanent visit to the vet. But I guess that is a typical reaction all patients have from time to time to their analysts.

8

But What If She Were in a Hospital?

All sin is a form of sickness. C. S. Lewis sometimes used the word *bent* to visualize sin. Sometimes sin leads to physical, emotional, or mental sickness beyond the spiritual disease.

When someone is ill from a disease, car accident, or other tragedy he or she is usually hospitalized. It is easy to understand that he is sick. Even though he may have caused his problem through carelessness or abuse, we think of him as legitimately sick and have a great deal of compassion on him and his family. We have a compartment in our mind for people who are not well and have developed customs to deal with them socially.

I look at my situation. There is a part of me that wants to "get on with my life" (whatever that means). The pain of trying again and again only to be rejected once more by her is crippling. Should I hold her accountable for her decisions? Is she responsible for her actions?

Her choices and other factors argue that there is much more at work here. She is different in so many ways. What is involved seems to me to be much more than just a broken marriage with the typical painful consequences. I want to confront her adult to adult for what she is doing to me, to us, to the children, to so many people. I want her to stop it. I want to shake her and wake her from this bad dream.

But then I am reminded that the evidence is that maybe Anne is not well. How would I treat her if she were hospitalized? How would others treat us if she were "officially sick"?

I am especially torn when I swear at her picture or the thought of what she is doing to us. There is a real sense in which I do not hold my wife accountable for what she has chosen to do to us. I believe there may be some underlying cause. All broken relationships are sick, but my perspective draws me toward the conclusion that Anne is reacting to unresolved issues from her past that perhaps are surfacing now.

When my grandfather started to deteriorate mentally in his mid-eighties, I remember my grandmother's frustration. My grandfather would put the mail in the bread box and leave his watch under the sofa. He once gave my grandmother twenty dollars and thanked her for cleaning the apartment. She would from time to time get angry at him for doing these things. Then she remembered that this was not the Jack she had known as her husband for sixty-plus years.

I look at Anne and have many of the same conflicting feelings. It is as though the "Invasion of the Body-Snatchers" has taken place. She looks like my wife. She sounds like my wife. But she is not the woman I have known for over a decade. Someone has captured her. I wait for the ransom note, which, no matter what the price, I would pay. But it never comes. There is no way to reach her.

Since she is not institutionalized, people are not sure how to relate to her or to me. It is hard to describe. If one of us were in the hospital, others would be over with casseroles or dinners. A whole different support system would be put into action. Instead, we are a threat. If she were physically disabled, I would be angry at God for allowing that to have happened to her and to us. But eventually there would be some sense of "this is God's will for us." I could hang on so much better because there would not be the sense of her rejection of me. I ask myself again, "But what if she were in a hospital?"

9

Sorry, I've Got to Play It Again, Sam.

I am surprised by how much I have needed to talk to people. I knew before that conversation was a way of releasing stress. That, combined with all of the unanswerable questions brought on by this kind of problem, has turned me into a chatterbox. I keep thinking about that old proverb about empty vessels making a lot of noise.

When my crisis broke, I knew from my experience in working with others that I would be a basket case for quite a while. My need for people to talk to meant that I would require both time and energy from others.

Since most people already have a busy life, I chose a group of eight friends for support. I called them or got together for coffee on a regular basis. Most of them have had experience in dealing with people in crisis and understood the cost of sharing someone's pain.

As a new crisis would emerge or I would have a strange encounter with Anne, I would need to talk to someone. More than that, I would need to talk over and over again. It was very repetitious. There was something in the review of the small event over and over that helped me to cope. Most of the time, no magical answer or even logical explanation of the event was produced. But the process of talking helped to relieve some of the tension and to serve as a reality check for me.

Early in the pastorate, I had a young husband come to me after his wife had left him. I spent hours and hours with him as I listened, comforted, and prayed with him. It seemed to me that it took an incredible amount of time and energy. With all my other ministry load, it was threatening to burn me out. I realize now how little help I was compared to how much he needed to talk. The truth is that he needed eight of me to help him cope during his crisis. As with any grieving process, in a divorce or separation there is the need to revisit the loss over and over. That is why I decided that I would reduce the risk of burning out my relationships by leaning on a bunch of friends rather than just one or a few. Even so, it has been stressful for them.

There have been times that I have sensed (or imagined) that some have pulled back for a break. I am sure that seeing a phone message from Pat doesn't always bring them joy, but they keep listening, praying, talking, and caring. They have invested many hours, cups of coffee, phone bills, and emotions in sharing my burden. I thank God for them. I worry about other people who face a crisis with fewer resources than I have. How do their friends cope? How do they survive?

When I call one of my group, at times I want to start off my conversation with "Sorry, I've got to play it again, Sam."

10

"Count Your Blessings" and Other Nauseating Songs

When Anne was pregnant, she experienced some surprising changes in what foods she liked and disliked. She didn't have the proverbial cravings for chocolate-covered pickles or pizza and ice cream, but some of her favorite foods turned her off. She had a new appreciation for other foods. Her most requested craving was easy to order—Chinese food.

My separation has had a similar effect on my taste in music. Songs I used to enjoy or that at least never bothered me now make me ill. One of the worst offenders, a song that never bothered me before, is "Count Your Blessings." In some cases a song distresses me because of the words, but in this case it is the music. The words speak of being tempest tossed, discouraged, thinking all is lost—sentiments of people in pain. But when those words are linked with a bright and peppy tune it all sounds trite.

There are some songs of victory that give hope. The positive message is rooted in the final outcome of eternity. Hymns that recognize the pain, suffering, and injustice of the present evil age speak with a reality that people who are suffering know firsthand. But those same hymns announce that the age that is to come has begun and will ultimately triumph. It is that apocalyptic view that allows people to trust God in their pain.

In this individualistic society, which looks at everything from a personal point of view, it is difficult not to see one's problems in isolation. It is no comfort to realize that the statistics suggest that what I am going through is typical of people my age. I would have preferred to think that my marriage was immune to the pressures of our time. I have thought about diseases. Religious people run the same general risks of getting cancer, Alzheimer's, or heart disease as the population in general. That is part of being human, living in a world of sickness and disease. Though we would like to think of ourselves as immune, godly people who take care of their bodies still suffer disease and death.

We would hope, however, that our principles and perspectives would allow us to avoid the trends in divorce and other social ills. But the sad truth is that we are just as vulnerable to the sickness of sin as human beings still living only in this present evil age.

Although some songs have become repulsive in my present condition, others have become special friends. Songs such as "Be Still My Soul" and "Tears Are a Language God Understands" speak to me in my pain. "It Is Well with My Soul" is another hymn with that combination of honesty about suffering but ultimate victory. In a world that knows so much personal tragedy, we have an obligation to give a clear message of ultimate hope that does not minimize the sadness of the journey. "I Am Willing, Lord" and "Meet Me Here" reflect those profound emotions and contradictions.

Perspective on the entire picture, including the dark colors and the shadows, adds the dimension that enriches our ability to truly count our blessings.

11

Body, Soul, and Spirits

I broke a toe in high school when I was playing soccer. I didn't notice it when my foot collided with the other player (I saw his pain!) but as I went back to my position, my toe shouted "injury." Soon I couldn't walk. Then I couldn't stand. When I made it home, I felt as though my whole body hurt. Extreme pain focuses our attention.

My theology understands human beings as body, soul, and spirit. It is interesting to explore those different areas and how they contribute to who we are.

Sometimes in sports or in writing music one experiences a unity of being. All that one is, is in harmony, and there is a great sense of wholeness.

As I have gone through this separation, I have expected to get really sick. The stress, depression, anger, and pain have been so intense and constant that I figured I would be a great candidate for all sorts of bugs. (Then again, in my present state bugs might not dare come near me!) I did the prudent thing and added another $1 million of life insurance to make my death profitable if I did get really sick.

Early on in the separation, I went to see the doctor to have my blood pressure and heart checked. I also talked to him about the sleepless nights since Anne confirmed that she was not moving back home. He prescribed some sedatives to make sure that I had some sleep but was concerned that I not become dependent. The sedatives helped for the immediate weeks of the crisis. My counselor and doctor both said that the pain could only be deferred. I would have to face it at some point. The sooner I allowed the suffering to do its work, the sooner I would begin to recover from the initial separation shock. I was able to throw a few pills in that prescription away. As the counselor and the doctor predicted, the pain was waiting for me.

Whether it was good genes or the extra adrenaline from stress, I did not feel physically terrible most of the time. That was in spite of too little sleep, a lack of appetite, and personal turmoil.

Maybe it is the sense of helplessness that is the worst for me. I have only two choices: to act out against Anne or to tolerate my circumstances as best I can. I have had sufficient grace from God in my contacts with her to avoid the regrettable scenes that so often characterize separated spouses. But the powerlessness is so strange.

On one occasion during my nightly phone calls to the kids my son was crying and upset. Jeff was reaching out for me to help him. Here I was, five minutes away by car but as good as worlds away. Jeff and Laura seemed like hostages who also had no choices. He was hurting and I could do nothing to help him. Why should he suffer? Anne's words about how this separation was the best thing for the children as well as for her and me echoed in my mind. What kind of father was I? My five-year-old son was suffering because of us, and I could do nothing to help. I felt like a failure.

I went out and bought a bottle of fine red wine. I popped the cork and sat down and polished off the bottle in half an hour. I had never been drunk before. Apparently a good wine will have the same effect as a bottle of the cheap stuff. Either way, that bottle will not be remembered as vintage of a good year. After falling asleep right away, I woke up a couple of hours later. It took about half an hour to figure out how to stand up. Once up, I couldn't stand for any length of time. It was much like playing a video game with the joystick off-center. Every move I thought I was making in one direction did not get me there. I have a new appreciation of where the walls and furniture in my apartment are located. My dog saw my strange gait and decided that it was a good idea to hide under the bed. After a visit to the bathhroom, I sat back down in my chair. I was physically helpless.

But my body was not without its options. It decided to do a good 1960s-style protest for being treated this way. I felt a sudden rush from the center of my being and watched as I projected my thoughts all over the floor. What a mess. I tried to get to the couch to change positions.

I called a couple of friends to share the moment. They have been so patient. After a couple more hours and a couple more "demonstrations," I got upstairs to bed and spent the night feeling as though I was going to die—or worse, that I wouldn't.

When I awoke the next morning my body had a new appreciation of how my soul and spirit had been feeling since Anne left. It was not a recommended way to find out.

12

Clichés, Platitudes, and Other Ice-breakers

One of my friends, Kenny, and I have a standing joke about clichés and platitudes. Whenever we are together for our weekly coffee, he will always find a spot or two to throw in a truism. We both laugh.

Kenny knows that clichés are an attempt to answer questions that have no human answers. I enjoy the moment because it reminds me of how often we must fall back on trite sayings to fill the uncomfortable silences in our questions.

Unlike Kenny, other persons I know have used clichés as a goad or a corrective. When they tell me to "Just trust God," "Confess sin in your life," or "Let God get your attention," or when they remind me that a husband "should love his wife as Christ loved the church," they think they have done their duty. Now it is up to me.

Part of our reaction to people in pain is understandable. What do we say when we see people struggling? How do we explain the effects of broken people in a broken world? We all find silence uncomfortable.

It has been said that Job's friends were doing all right until they started to talk. There is a sense in which the silent presence of a friend during grief says much and really comforts.

Still, I value the clichés and platitudes. They are often "truth statements" that describe life and God's participation in it. There are obviously good clichés and poor ones. Some are clearly wrong theologically. But I still need to hear people reassure me of God's continuing love and faithfulness. In my pain, when I feel as though God is not there or that He has abandoned me, it is the presence of His people who can speak to me.

Clichés such as the ones my friend Kenny uses help most when I know that the other person really understands that I am in pain and that there are no easy answers. When a platitude is not used to avoid the reality of a problem or to end that part of the conversation it can be helpful. Like all good preaching, it is a restatement of the ideal and serves as a challenge to me to keep on keeping on (oops—a cliché slipped in there).

13

Looking for the Pony

One of the Morgan regulars is Bing, a former pastor of mine. When Anne prepared and gave me a list of "your friends and my friends" to identify who was supporting us during the separation, he had the misfortune of being on both lists. It is a testimony to his people skills that he managed that feat, although it is a bit like a "good news/bad news" joke. The good news is that you made both lists; the bad news is that you have to deal with both of us.

Bing is an optimist by nature. Though not as out of touch with reality as my inborn optimism makes me, he still has a bad dose of that personality defect.

During one of our conversations he recounted an old joke that has been a quintessential part of our situation. The story is told of a city family going to the country to visit relatives on the farm. When they get there, the tour of the farmyard begins. In the cow barn is a huge pile of manure. The little city boy runs to the pile and starts to plow through it, searching desperately. His parents are horrified and shout,

"Johnny, what are you doing?" He replies, "With a pile this big, there's got to be a pony in here somewhere!"

As the pile of life-circumstances has grown for me, I have found myself "looking for the pony" too. There is enough here to suggest that a team of Clydesdales is present! Sometimes it is trying to see the positive in a particular development. Other times, it is part of looking for some ultimate good to come from this mess. Believe me, that takes imagination!

Another friend, Jerry, has pointed out that one of my problems is that in spite of many negative life experiences, I have not yet figured out that life is usually not a pleasant experience. I have tended to forget the bad and remember the good. In other hopeless situations I have hung on to the very end. I don't give up on important areas of life easily. Like the captain on a sinking ship already twenty feet below the surface, I have to be tapped on the shoulder and reminded on that maybe it is time to abandon ship.

Part of my optimism is due to my worldview, which has hope as a major component. Maybe I am optimistic because I have seen many "impossible" problems solved. Maybe it is my self-image. One test the counselor used indicated I was in the top 3 percent of the population in self-image. The test indicated that "this person's motto is—'If you know me, you'll like me. If you don't like me, it's because you don't know me —but you will like me when you get to know me.'" Whatever the origin, my attitude certainly sets me up for a surprise when I am rejected.

My optimism could come from my Scottish heritage. A king of Scotland, Robert the Bruce, and his army had endured six defeats in battle. Discouraged, the king and some of his men hid in a cave. There they watched a spider trying to begin a web by swinging across from one wall to the other. Six times the spider tried, but failed. On the seventh try, the persistent spider succeeded. Robert the Bruce took that as a sign for him to try once more to win the battle. He rallied his men and succeeded. So maybe my optimism is a flaw in my genes.

Whatever the reason, I continue to look for reasons to hope. There have been no concrete signs. In fact, Anne has made clear from the beginning that the marriage is over. To my knowledge, she has not allowed herself any doubt. But I keep looking for the pony in this mess.

14

Free Will Versus the Sovereignty of God —My Choice

Since my wife decided to leave, I have felt powerless. Anne has not been open to any discussion of reconciliation from the beginning. All my prayers have not changed her mind.

I just want God to intervene. I appeal to God to exercise His sovereignty. But whenever I mention the sovereignty of God, I am quickly reminded of the balancing truth of free will. I know that God has chosen to show great respect for our freedom to choose.

Our choices often impact many other people and even generations. It is an awesome responsibility. In our small choices we set ourselves up for the big ones. When we reach those big decisions, the notion of being faithful in little things certainly can be seen in how we manage our relationships.

Since Anne chose to leave and I have worked on reconciliation for the past year, it feels as though she has the "free will" and I am stuck with the "sovereignty of God." I wish it were the other way around. Oh, I could have exercised my free will in being miserable with her or in "getting on with my life" by initiating a divorce and starting a new relationship. But that is not what I really long for. I want this fracture to mend. But it has not been my choice.

As I lie awake at four in the morning, calling out to God in my tears, I want Him to exercise His sovereignty.

"Now would be fine. Go ahead, God. I know that You can do it. You can move mountains. You can heal the sick. I believe. Yes, I believe. No, I don't prefer a particular method —You choose, God. Uh, as long as it isn't one that takes a lot of time. You see, I have waited as long as I can. I have been very patient. No, I don't want anything really bad to happen to her. No, I wouldn't like the children to be really sick or (gulp!) die. But I know that You are not that kind of God. No, I was thinking more of a lullaby to calm her down, than a zap.

"What if Your sovereignty demands more time because she isn't ready to listen yet? Could You sing to her a little louder? How about moving someone into her life who could give her a nudge in the right direction? And at least take away the people who are a negative influence. Yes, You can zap them. Oh, that's right, not a good attitude. Maybe just a little zap?

"And those people who are gloating over the 'Morgan mess'—how about a flu bug? I know, I know. Sorry.

"Some people say that You are teaching me through this, God. Others say that You are trying to get my attention. Let me be very clear here, Father. I think You have my attention. This is as focused as I can get. I didn't sign up for a grad course in suffering. I knew I spent too much time in the epistles of Peter. What's worse, I am not suffering 'for Christ's sake'—I am just suffering for being a sinner. Now there's a scary thought. What if this is to prepare me for something tougher? Oh, boy. There goes my blood pressure again. Was that the idea? Was it because You didn't trust me? Or am I supposed to learn what an emotional straitjacket feels like? I wish the walls were at least padded here, God. I keep bruising myself.

"Your sovereignty is real, God. But I am still trying to figure out—is this Your discipline for me as Your child or am I just a victim of the percentages? Is it both? I wish I knew for sure whether it is really over. At times, my head is quite sure that she is never coming back to our marriage. But I am not sure.

"Do You remember watching us when Anne was having an ultrasound when our daughter was on the way? We were good sports about not knowing whether it was a boy or girl. But I need to know how this will turn out. You can give it to me straight, God: Is it terminal? But I suppose that even if You said yes, that would not preclude the possibility of a resurrection.

"What does Gothard call it—death of a vision? Oh, oh. Maybe I haven't let go enough and trusted Your sovereignty. How do I let go?

"But if our marriage is like Christ and His church, You never give up on us. You keep loving Your church in spite of our unfaithfulness. I believe that my vows were for unconditional love. There were no strings attached. There were no easy escape clauses. It doesn't help that I am a hopeless romantic and optimist, God. What a terrible time to be idealistic.

"Well, You know, God, how I am feeling. Thanks for this talk. I guess I should remember that my free will is to submit to Your sovereignty as best I can. And Your sovereignty will ultimately overrule Anne's free will. But if I could make just one more suggestion . . ."

15

The Faithful Few

It takes courage to help people in pain. Doctors, nurses, and counselors all know the cost of giving as part of their job. A special kind of commitment and willingness to take risks is necessary.

I will be eternally grateful for the people God has used during my crisis. Someone in this degree of turmoil does not make for pleasant or easy conversation. This is the one section of the book where I am tempted to name the people who have hung in there with me. They are all “hall-of-famers.” It has been interesting to see the mix of the group. Some, like Charles, my roommate from college, or my business partner, Jerry, have been the “thick and thin” kind of friend. (I am still not sure whether this is the thick or the thin—probably both.)

Others include a former pastor, a professor from college, a pastoral colleague, a current pastor and denominational leader. Then there are a couple of old friends from my teenage days at a camp and a friend from the church I had pastored.

Family have been there in a different way. Anne's brother, who was a childhood friend from camp, has maintained regular contact.

As soon as my crisis broke, I immediately called a number of these people and asked for their help. With my experience in the pastorate helping people through this kind of crisis, I knew the enormous drain that a person in need could be on others. Too often, people turn to one or two friends and burn them out in a short time. I have said to some in my support group that they should imagine my level and frequency of contact with them and multiply it by eight to know something of the amount of time and patience I have used up. The cost to them in time, strength, coffee, and phone bills is humbling. (I should have bought stock in the phone company when this started.) They are a powerful reminder of their and God's love for me.

All in their own way have kept me going through this time. I would like to speak of some of the many things they have done that have helped me.

Unconditional acceptance of me as a person has been a common denominator. That is not to suggest that my friends believe that "I'm right and she's wrong," or that Anne and I have not both contributed to our problems. In some cases, I have shared the gory details, but in others I have shared less of our past. All in my support group have had in common an approach that looked not so much on the past but on what I was willing to do in the present. In counseling, that seems to be the bottom line. The past can help someone begin to understand the history of his problems, but it is all irrelevant if a person is not willing to work on the future. A meaningful joke has been, "How many psychiatrists does it take to change a light bulb? One—but the light bulb must be willing to change." Caring unconditionally has given me the courage to keep talking.

Regular contacts have been essential. In the loneliness, isolation, and confusion of this time, the willingness of my friends to have that weekly or biweekly coffee or phone call has made all the difference. I thank God for the faithful few.

16

Learning How to Fall

Our five-year-old son has been learning how to ice skate. It takes a lot of courage for Jeff to try it and for me to watch it. Those thin blades are supposed to keep him up. One wonders about the sanity of the person who invented the sport—probably a frustrated engineer seeking revenge on the masses.

After a few falls, it is time talk about falling. As in most sports, Jeff will fall down. How he lands can make a big difference. It is hard not to associate skating and headaches when you fall.

So we spent some time practicing how to fall and not bump your head. "Keep your head up once you feel like you're going to fall. Let your shoulders feel the ice. Don't be afraid to roll a bit. Most of all, get back up. Daddy will be there to help pick you up."

After practicing a few times, Jeff started "to fall better." It was easier to get back up because he was not crying from a bumped noggin. He became more willing to skate harder and longer because he wasn't afraid of falling.

As I watched, it occurred to me that we do not learn how to fall spiritually, mentally, or emotionally. We teach the fact that we will fall often, but we spend little time understanding what to do when we are falling to minimize the damage. I know many people who never seem to get back up after a fall. They broke too many "bones" when they went down. Who is there to help them get their balance again?

How do we fall spiritually? How do we keep our heads up when we are going down? Why do we get back up?

Having watched others go through the experience of separation and having had other failures in my life experience, I had learned a few things about falling. When my wife left, I felt myself losing balance, and I knew that I would be grounded very soon. For that reason I sought out friends to help me get back up. I told them I was falling. That honesty was necessary for me not to hit the ground with full force. The arms of my friends helped to break my fall a bit.

It also helped to decide to be honest with God and myself by admitting the pain and the emotions. I was not going to pretend that I had not fallen.

Then I eliminated all areas of ministry as quickly as possible. That was primarily to restate to my wife that my priorities of God first, family second, and ministry third really were my value system and that working out our marriage problems would get my full attention. A second benefit was that it allowed me to deal with my pain honestly. Although it was tempting to keep doing ministry with all of the support systems involved, that would have led me to deny the extent of the problem. I was going to need to be a taker and not a giver for a while, and that was OK.

Ultimately, I had to be willing to get back up. There is a lot of risk in doing that. Getting back up means that you can fall again. It is hard to fall off the ground. But there are other dangers to staying down. Like my son, who could be struck by another skater if he stayed down, I would be vulnerable to more and different problems if I gave up.

There are certainly times when I wonder why I keep trying to stand again. I have hit the ground many times in the process of attempting to get back on my feet. Perhaps it has been my hope in God, or His grace at work in me, that has made it possible for me to keep making an effort. The support of friends who believe in me and have encouraged me to get up was real. Maybe it has been wanting to be there for the children. Or maybe it has been a true love that wants to be ready for reconciliation if that is possible. I am sure that I will continue to have more practice learning how to fall.

17

Beware of Master

Some canines can be excellent watchdogs. Other dogs, like mine, have a very precise contract. Toffee barks and protects the house if one of us is home. Otherwise, she hides under the bed. When our matrimonial house was for sale, many of the real estate agents said that they were relieved that the listing was wrong. When I asked why, they told how they were fearful of dogs and expected to meet one at our house. I told them that there really was a dog but that she barked only when we were home. It was not in her contract to protect the house alone.

As I go through this time of separation from the woman I love, the many moods and emotions I experience make me wonder if the dog ever needs to do the barking.

There are times when I do not want to answer the phone. A knock at the door makes my heart race. Is it a process server with the divorce papers from her? Is it a visitor who is able to accept me and my new "single-again" house as they find it? Will they judge me because it is not the spotless, beautifully decorated home that Anne always kept? She had such great taste. It felt so secure to know that one area of my life could be ordered, no matter how confusing business or ministry might be.

Now, in a split second, that knock reminds me of all that is not and may never be again.

I long to be with caring people. But my reserves are so low. Will I have the energy to face someone I have not seen for a while? I wish people would call before they come over. Even five minutes would do. Part of it is to fix up the house, but part of it is to fix up my emotions. I spend so much time thinking, crying, and praying. But I don't want them to avoid coming over. There have been so few people. It reinforces how much has changed.

My mind races to the many times my anger has seethed when I am downtown. As I think of my circumstances, it would be the wrong time for a mugger to choose me. Come on—give me an excuse to fight. I wonder how many of the members of the French Foreign Legion had joined to forget a woman? No wonder they fought so well.

O God. It is another knock. It is 8:30 in the morning. I have been up all night tossing and turning as I have wrestled with my demons. They knock again. I come down from upstairs. Toffee is barking. I have not showered. I am wearing a bathrobe. As I look through the opaque glass I see two shapes. *Oh, no—police? Process servers? I can't take any more stress. Why do they have to invade my life right now? Why so early in this already long day?* I open the door unconscious of how I look. I figure it must be quite a sight by their reaction. The two ladies say good morning. *It's the cults! Ugh! Just what I don't need this morning!*

One woman begins her machine-gun speech. Imagine these words said without a pause or breath taken: "Do you know that many people believe that there will be peace in the world and there will be harmony but that there will never be peace and the end of the world is coming in ways and sooner than anyone can imagine but we know what is going to happen." I asked her, "What religion are you?" She answered with her group's name.

In happier times, I would have identified myself as a pastor of my denomination. That would usually finish the conversation quickly. Instead, I borrow from J. R. R. Tolkien's description in *Lord of the Rings* of the time Gandalf met the evil Balrog. I raise my hands and look into the woman's eyes and say in ominous tones, "I am a servant of the secret fire—you cannot pass." A dread sweeps over them. They turn and run down the sidewalk. I imagine what their sharing time will be like when they report to their group the bizarre experience they have had with the strange man in the old house.

I think then that I should buy a "Beware of Dog" sign and cross out the word *dog* and make it read, "Beware of Master—Separated from His Wife."

18

Alzheimer's Please!

When Anne and I finally reconcile, we are walking by the sea on a bright summer day. Hand-in-hand we laugh and talk. We are one. There is a new depth in our being. There is a richer quality to who we are. I love her so much and she loves me. Our separation is a faded mist. I am so thankful God has done this miracle. *Thank You, God. Thank, You God.*

I sit up with a start. *O God. No, no. It can't just be a dream. It is so real. Let me sleep, God. Let me return to my Loth Lorien where there is no time or evil.* I begin to shake. I can't stop. I sweat. My eyes well up with tears. I begin to sob. I can't stop crying. *God, where is the hope! Why do You have to torment me like this?*

How often have I drifted into the world of dreams with us together this year. Sleep is not a safe place anymore. It is a time when memories become dreams. Dreams become hope. But hope is shattered by reality.

I remember when I used to sleep well. Eight blissful hours beside her. Peace. Contentment. Comfort. Oneness.

Safety. Now those same hours haunt me. I am visited by my demons each night. They torment me. They prod me. They slice me. I am not sure which dreams are worse. Some dreams are of reconciliation. Others are of Anne's being with another man—some I know, some I don't. I even had a dream where I was attending her wedding. It repeated three times that night. *O God, it hurts.*

Memory is one of God's greatest gifts to us. It can also be one of His greatest curses. So many happy memories together can bring a smile and a tear at the same time. So much has been lost. When will this bleeding stop? *O God, it hurts.*

There are the memories of her as she was—happy, caring, taking, giving. The sparkle is in her eye. That was her nickname, you know. I called her Sparkle. Her eyes danced like a fairy princess. I loved to look into her deep brown eyes. They were so expressive and soft. They were bright and alive. Her smile would warm all who saw it. She had a magnetism and a virtue that radiated from her. People were put at ease and knew that they were important. She was someone who expressed hospitality and mercy with such ease and grace.

One of our friends described her as a "storybook person." She went on to describe how Anne was such an interesting person to be with. She was so effective in ministry. She could express herself well. Organization came easily to her. Although very much her own person, she was a great wife, mother, homemaker. Superb in business settings, she could mix with the pauper or the elite on Wall Street. Young or old, learned or fools—all experienced her sincere love and care. I was so proud of her. I often called her my better "three-quarters" instead of my better half (which with her slim figure could only be interpreted one way). I felt so blessed that we were married and in love.

My last conversation with my grandfather as he neared death while Anne and I were dating was on how much he liked Anne. "She's a good one—keep her." *Oh, Grandpa—*

what should I do? I want to be a little boy again going with you for a walk by the harbor and watch the ships. Oh, Grandpa, tell me what to do. Please fix it for me.

Waves of memories flood over me. *I miss her so much, God.* Now she hates me. I want to forget. But they were good times. No matter what she says. But it hurts to remember. Maybe memory loss is a blessing when you get old. That's it. I have a new prayer request. I'll order up a disease. *God, Alzheimer's please!*

19

Bless the Beasts and the Children

Karen Carpenter sang the song "Bless the Beasts and the Children" from the book of the same title. It spoke of a desire for blessing on the animals and the children since they have no voice or choice. They are vulnerable and so dependent. Often, they are victims of another's choices.

One of the especially painful experiences in this separation has been to see our children suffer. Anne says that this has been for the best for them. They spend more "quality time" with their dad than ever before. It is all very typical "leaver" talk.

My former relationship with the children has been characterized by Anne as "reading them a story and tucking them in at night." Like most things she describes from our marriage, I don't recognize the family she is talking about.

My life has always been centered on Anne and the children. Apart from my relationship with God, nothing in this life has meant more to me.

One of the hardest moments in my life came when I met with my counselor early in the separation. She told me that in order to have the best chance to reconcile with Anne, I must not make the children an issue. I was clear on my priorities. Anne came first and the kids were a close second. It was in the best interests of the children, Anne, and me to reconcile. So as Anne announced what the children's schedule and routines would be, I had to bite my tongue and acquiesce. She imposed the new world order on us.

Within this set of constraints, I had to redefine my relationship with the children. I was initially with them every Friday and Saturday. Anne left just before Christmas, so I had an extended time with the kids in those early weeks.

It was tough to deal with my own grief and shock as well as their confusion. Everything was so wrong. I had to be tough for them. No, I had to be real for them. The tears were real—both mine and theirs. Our son, Jeff, was most verbal as he tried in his four-year-old mind to make sense of something that I could not as an adult process. Comforting the children was excruciating for me. *What have I done to them? They may never know a normal life again. Why can't I fix it? O God, where is Your mercy?*

All the questions that they asked cried "Ouch." Why isn't Mommy here? When is she coming home? Why is Mommy angry? Why are you crying, Daddy? Do you still love Mommy? Does Mommy still love you? I want everyone to be together again. All the family. I'm scared, Daddy. Will you still love me? Will you always take care of me? Does Mommy still love us? Daddy, where's Mommy?

Where is the Anne I knew?

I can understand why fathers often resort to one of the extremes—forget the family and run, or grab the kids and run. Each contact is full of pain—even the joyful ones. The children are the real victims in this. They had no choice. They have no voice.

My primary goal was to increase my level of contact with the children. A week is a long time when you are two years old. So, with Anne's agreement, I call the children every night at a specified time. No matter where I am on business or travel, the children know that the phone ringing at 7:00 P.M. is Daddy. These calls can be really tough. Each time is a reminder that life is fractured for us. I try to put aside the pain and let the kids know that they are the most important people in my life. Our son has started to learn jokes, so one of my tasks is to have a "joke of the day" for Jeff. It's neat!

I have committed to Anne from the beginning that I would take the children whenever there was extra time available. So if they were sick, if she needed a baby-sitter, if she was going on vacation, or if she needed time out—I would be there if at all possible. There have been times when I have canceled a week's appointments at short notice to gain extra time.

After going to court on custody six months after Anne left, my schedule changed to every second week for a four-day weekend. I take each of those Thursdays and Fridays off to be with them, and I do not get any baby-sitters during those four days. We are together the whole time.

Each week they receive a letter from me. In addition to a short note, there is often a copy of a picture from our vacation together. I also began a sticker collection with them from the cartoon characters Chip 'n' Dale. I enclose a package of stickers, which they stick in a collector's book. It creates expectations but also demonstrates to them my commitment. I have also subscribed to some children's magazines, which they receive at Anne's.

When our son began kindergarten, I volunteered to be a teacher's helper every other Thursday morning during the week that I do not see the children. Anne has not been happy about that, but it has been a significant time for me and our son. Sadly, it aggravates our daughter, Laura, because she knows on a Thursday that Jeff will see me and she will not. All of my attempts to have time with Laura in the off-week have been refused by Anne, as she cites that transitions are too difficult for the children. I wonder if it doesn't have more to do with her being in control.

In spite of all of my efforts, these extra times are a poor substitute for a daily relationship with the children. When Anne explains to Laura that the reason that Daddy is not with them is that "He has to work" I want to scream. How does she dare to communicate that my work is more important than my daughter? What kind of view of fathers and work will she have? It all stinks.

I think about the fact that almost half of the country's children must endure this kind of experience. What kind of world is being created in the next generation? The children suffer so much. They have no voice. They have no choice. *We all need Your help, God. Especially, bless the beasts and the children.*

20

The Right and Left

Those who do the leaving have a very definite set of explanations and rationalizations to show that they are right in their choice. I call these the "Rights." They will tell you how much better life is for everyone, including the spouse who has been left. In my case, Anne says that "maybe Pat will meet someone who will make him happy." There seems to be very different worldviews and reactions. When I meet someone who is separated or divorced, one of the first questions that comes to mind is "Are they the Right or the Left?" I have little patience with the Rights.

I have observed that Rights have some common themes: marriage was death; divorce is freedom. The religious leavers also find all sorts of "proofs" that God agrees with their decision. In Anne's case, she cited that God blessed her decision by giving her a friend's home to live in (thanks, friends), an old car from her sister (part of "our family doesn't have any problems"), a job as a day-care worker (in a job market crying for day-careworkers), a new church (new group of caring people and friends who take her story at face value), and eventually an apartment. Since God had provided this new world, God supported her decision to leave.

Over the year, she has had a very difficult relationship with the family that initially took her in, totaled the car, is apparently not getting along well at work, and is in the process of finding a new "caring" church. Somehow, the same theology that "proves" that God is blessing is not applied to even the same things when they do not support one's choices. That is not unique to leavers; we all do it. But Rights have a lot to justify, so they are especially practiced at it.

The Lefts seem to have different reactions to the rejection that is the basic message given by the spouse who left. In my case, I alternate between feelings of terrible guilt and righteous anger at Anne's injustice. The guilt comes when I think about all of the times and ways I let her down. I could have been a better husband and father in so many areas. The "if onlys" play over and over. At other times, the horrible sense of unfairness takes over. It was not so bad. In fact, she had it pretty good. I was a good husband and father. How could she do such a thing to me?

I suppose that, as is the case with most people, the truth for me is somewhere in between. I had and have weaknesses as a person, husband, and father. I believe that I have used this time to improve myself in all those areas. As a husband, I have been limited in how I could express that to Anne. In the other areas, she probably does not know (or care?) about the progress I have made. She was not willing to give me a chance. As she said in her affidavit, "His promises were hollow and insincere." For that statement and the attitude it represents, I can and will be justifiably angry at her. But the circular arguments we make to ourselves but never to each other are part of being in the cross fire on the Left and the Right.

21

In-laws and Out-laws

Family systems are extremely complex. To try to understand why individuals react in a certain way is tough enough. To watch one set of family members react to problems is to see a strange mix of similarities and differences.

In dealing with a marriage breakdown, I would talk of in-laws or out-laws. The marriage of two people joins two families. In our case, there were many similarities when it came to spiritual values and commitment. But the ways that the families interacted among their members were very different. Those differences were accentuated by the separation.

Many truisms, such as "Blood is thicker than water," express the fact that each of us gives allegiance to his own family. I understand that. Those support systems help us define ourselves and cope in times of crisis.

In our crisis, I have seen a wide range of reactions from both families. It is not an easy time for the extended families in such turmoil. There is the natural wish to believe the best about one's own child and to doubt one's child-in-law. Particularly when the separation occurs in a religious context, all of the stigma felt by the separating spouses now attaches to some extent to the families. Parents begin to question what role they had in the breakup. They feel it personally.

In my case, my relationship with Anne's brothers predated my knowing Anne. We had been campers and later counselors together at a summer camp since the age of eight. Since it was segregated as boys' camps in July and girls' camps in August, we met brothers not sisters until one was old enough to work on staff in the other month. Anne worked first in the kitchen staff in boys' camp as she was finishing secondary school. A summer later, we began to date. My brothers also knew her brothers on the same basis, so there was some preblending of the two families already underway.

Since the separation, I have had contact with only one of Anne's family. We have continued to have some business projects together and have kept in touch. It has been tough for him since Anne has insisted that people make a choice between their relationship with her or with me. It is painful to add those other relationships to the losses.

My brothers both tried to reach out to Anne. One brother and his wife had dinner with her early in the separation. My parents also tried to express their interest in Anne by sending occasional cards, and they spoke with her by phone on a couple of occasions. In our family's case, they are grieving their own loss of a family member. In our family system, Anne was never a hyphenated relative. She was valued and accepted as a member of the Morgan clan. They have gone through the stages of separation trauma as they have had to watch me and the children struggle.

I have experienced my own sense of loss from her family as well. It makes one question what kind of relationship existed before the separation. What kind of relationship exists between the other in-law children and the family? My attempts to reach out to Anne's father have been unanswered.

I believed that we had enjoyed an excellent relationship. I had respected him very much.

There is no question that in times of crisis, it is normal and helpful for families to close ranks to support a wounded member. No one would expect a parent not to support his or her child. Yet I question whether it is right in all circumstances for that line of support to be crossed to the point that the child believes or is told that his parents agree with whatever choice he makes, or is automatically told that his choice is justified. Surely there are instances where a parent needs to rise above the fray and make clear that though he loves his child unconditionally, he opposes his decision. Certainly a parent should hear both sides of a problem before making any pronouncements. Ultimately, grown children make their own choices and face the consequences. Often parents can do little more than listen and pray. But perhaps those are the best responses.

I do not envy parents and other family members who try to cope with the separation of their children. Perhaps those wonderful qualities of grace and wisdom need extra attention during this stressful time, as they must encounter their own emotions and their strong feelings of their children, too.

Separation does not just rupture a couple, it explodes two families. It may be uncomfortable for parents and siblings to reach out to "the other side," but life seldom gives us easy choices. For the sake of the children who are also grandchildren and great-grandchildren of a relationship of which they are a permanent reminder, everyone needs to be in-laws, not out-laws.

22

Mirror on the Wall, Who's the Craziest of Them All?

As I have heard Anne and others describe her view of our marriage and my relationship with our children, I figure that one of us must be crazy. The marriage and husband that she describes are not the ones that I knew.

I know that two people often have different perceptions of what happened in their experiences. Especially traumatic situations seem to amplify our differences. But I find it troubling that many of our friends have expressed confusion when they have spoken to Anne and to me. Some believe that one of us must be lying. Others have given up trying to figure out "the truth." Many would just rather not hear about what happened.

It has been frustrating for me to sort out. I have tried to assume that I did not understand Anne. My heart wants to believe that she is wrong. My head tells me that we all have blind spots and misperceptions. I really want to know what upset her so much that she believed she needed to leave.

From the beginning of the separation, Anne would not talk to me about the marriage. She did not want to reconcile, so why talk about our decade together? As the year has passed, Anne has on a very few occasions talked with me about her perception of life with me. More often that information has been conveyed through third parties who have filtered her comments through their grid.

When people ask me about specific things that Anne has said I never quite know how to respond. Do I say, "There is her view, my view, and the truth"? Do I try to give my version of events or statements? How do I give my view without their then asking how I account for the differences in her story and mine.

With very few exceptions, I believe that Anne believes what she is saying. She says what she does with conviction. She is sincere. My dilemma is that I believe she is sincerely wrong with regard to many of the "facts" she reports. On things that were not matters of perception (where people would always differ) but of fact, I have tried to do reality checks with people who were present or knew firsthand.

I certainly can see that there were many things Anne felt or believed that I did not understand. I wish that I had been more perceptive. Did she really try to communicate them to me? Was I so slow to hear? Perhaps the best perspective came from Bobby, one of the "Morgan regulars," who said that he did not care to know about all of the issues of the past. To him what was important was what Anne and I were willing to do from that point on. There are times that I expect to hear a voice saying (with the appropriate background music), "Pat Morgan has gone on a journey. It is to a place where there is no time or space . . . where the world of nightmares has become reality. . . . He has entered the twilight zone." Rod Serling, is that you? Mirror, Mirror on the wall, who's the craziest of them all? I guess the answer is that we both are. You have to be crazy to be in this mess.

23

The World Through Smoke-colored Glasses

When I was in college, I was required to take a couple of courses in science. I chose geology. I had not studied it before and thought it would be an interesting change from the other science courses I had taken in high school.

It was fascinating. So many things that had been all around me but that I had only been vaguely aware of now became clear. I had begun to understand why things were the way that they were. A new appreciation began of the forces at work in shaping and changing the world I saw. Peneplains and extrusive rocks had always been there—I had just never noticed.

Since Anne left, I have come to see the social world in new ways. Unlike the sixties' perspective of looking at life through rose-colored glasses, my lenses are now smoke-colored. I had thought of myself as a sensitive person who was perceptive of other people's pain. But now I realized how little I really knew.

My education began with visits to the park with the children on a Saturday. We had gone there many times before the separation. But now, as I looked around, I saw the people in the park with new eyes. They were parents with children. But they were also more specifically single parents with children.

As I talked with different individuals, I found that almost all of the parents were separated or divorced. They were having their access time with their children. On their faces was etched an all too familiar pain. They were trying to cope. They were fighting not to become merely "significant others" in their children's lives.

How blind I had been. I guess we all see the world as we see ourselves. My thoughts went back to the many times I had been to the park. As I reflected, I had rarely seen two parents with their children. It is true that some of the parents were married, but most of them were probably struggling with a terrible loss.

Now, as I drive on a Saturday or Sunday, if I see a father with children I no longer assume that Mommy is at home reading or baking pies. It is more likely that the father is one of a growing number of people who have the horrible disease of being single again. Few of those parents seem to be happy with their fate, even those who have been able to "get on with their lives."

Our oil furnace needed some work. The technician came over during a day when the children were with me. He asked if I was baby-sitting. I explained that my wife had left. He began to pour out his own tale of his fifty-year-old wife's leaving him after thirty years of marriage for a guy who was his son's age. With the usual blend of anger and sadness, he told of the damage her decision had made in their family. Looking away, he spoke of how many friends he had known who had been divorced and how often he had told them to "get on with your life." Only now did he understand how lonely life could be. Even after two years, he struggled with what he had said to those friends. He said that his wife had tried to come back, but he could not stand the fear of losing her again. He told me that he had met a great lady and that they plan to be married in the summer. He ended by saying, "But I can't help still loving my ex. I do love her still."

There is a common bond and sensitivity for those touched by my affliction. You can't look at the world the same way again. I am doomed to see the world through smoke-colored glasses.

24

The Worst Kind of Heart Attack

I grew up in a home where my mother was a nurse. For a number of years, she worked in coronary and intensive care. I remember her description of the effect of a heart attack on people. During their recovery and even years later, many of these people who had experienced that terrifying "kick in the chest" had real changes in their emotional makeup. Those changes often lasted throughout the rest of their lives. Men who had been very traditional and out of touch with themselves emotionally found it easy to cry. They could empathize and reach out to others in ways they never could before.

It seems that the life experiences we face tend either to soften or to toughen us (or maybe a combination of both). We are softened toward the pain of others and are toughened in our own suffering.

This separation is that kind of experience for me. It is the worst kind of heart attack. My heart is broken and continues to hurt without any relief. I remember over and over the kick in the chest I felt the night Anne left. Even after all this time, the pain is just as intense whenever I think about it. In the earliest weeks, all I could think about was that pain. Now, it is never far away and can burst uninvited into my thoughts and feelings. It is like removing six layers of skin as a way of developing sensitivity. It works, but it is not a pleasant method.

I have faced new depths of emotion that are hard to describe. Before the separation I would not have described myself as an emotional person. Now new openings have been cut into my being and have given me a new understanding of who I am. The range of emotions has also been strange. I can go from feelings of euphoria to despair in a matter of moments with no particular cause.

Many people who have had a counseling or people focus in their ministry experience have the counselor's paranoia. It is based on 2 Corinthians 1:3-8. In that passage, Paul begins with an exhortation and blessing that praises "the God of all comfort, who comforts us in all our troubles, so that we can comfort" others with the comfort we have received. It is hard for people in counseling not to wonder that a given experience of personal pain is not part of the equipping to be more effective in ministering to others. It makes them want to say to God, "No. I don't want to learn what this feels like. I didn't sign up for a graduate degree in suffering. I knew I spent too much time in 1 Peter . . ."

I hate what this separation has done to me. I feel as though I continue to bleed all over. Cruelly, rather than letting me bleed to death, someone keeps giving me transfusions. That means I must keep going. The pain just keeps coming.

I am a more emotional person now. I hope that this experience does not eventually harden me into a bitter person. I worry about that. It is tempting to allow my anger to take over and cauterize my feelings toward Anne. I know that process can work. But it seems that I would have to give up a lot to make that exchange work.

I guess that I must keep facing the pain. Like the heart attack victim in the hospital, I have to start walking around again and rebuilding my strength. Some days seem better. Some are definitely worse. I don't want to give up hope. But there is so little that is hopeful here. This is the worst kind of heart attack.

25

Beggars Having the Rich to Dinner

Imagine a scene where a poor man invites a wealthy landowner for a meal. Think of the contradictions. What could the beggar offer the rich? It would be uncomfortable for the powerful to have to sit in the home of the poor. The rich man should be having the beggar to dinner.

Now carry that image from monetary wealth to social wealth. There are many poor people who have a healthy family situation. Many financially well-off people are in poverty in their family life.

As I think about how often and how many people we had into our home for a meal or an evening or a coffee, I now realize how rich we were. I did not recognize it at the time because I didn't understand how few people were in an environment where they were loved and felt safe. We had so much to give. Yet in spite of how much we shared, there were many people we missed.

Now I am in the social poorhouse. I sit in my silence and pain so all alone. As with most singles, widowed, or singles-again, I don't fit the social mix. People find it uncomfortable or unnatural to be around singles. They assume that singles are busy with their own activities.

In the case of the separated or divorced, there is the added dimension of not knowing what to say or do. How does one relate to them? Do they want to come over to one's home? Will seeing their friends in a family setting make their pain worse? Sometimes people are just too busy to notice the separated or divorced person or even to ask those questions. It is tough enough just to survive the hectic and stressful life each family must face.

One solution is to establish support group ministries to help them. Although the single or divorced person may value opportunities to meet with people facing the same crisis and may find it useful to discuss unique or common problems with people in similar difficulties, support group ministries are not the only answer. They are not substitutes for being accepted and included as a person. It is hard when you have been rejected by your spouse not to feel as though others are treating you like a castaway when they no longer include you in their social life. It is tough enough during the typical days, but at holiday times it is especially tough. This year instead of receiving five or six invitations to Christmas or other parties I had one. It is difficult to believe that that was a coincidence.

Perhaps the best help that can be given socially to the separated is to give him options. Give him the chance to say, "No thanks, not tonight." If you hear it once or twice, don't give up. It is probably not a statement about you or your hospitality. It may just be one of those days when he needs to hide in a bunker because he is feeling shell-shocked.

You cannot help everyone. But perhaps you can help one broken person during his time of despair. I don't expect that those who are there for me have any magic answers for my problems. I don't always want to discuss my separation, but sometimes I do. I value those friends who have given me the privilege of having the choice. Sitting with a family at their dinner table does bring pain. But it also reminds me that there are still families who are together. It says that I am OK enough to be included.

I have reached out to a number of people. Some have come to my home for dinner or have come to a restaurant or coffee shop. I wonder about all of the hurting people who cannot reach out. I am thankful for the friends who have been willing to come to visit. But let's not only make the beggars have the rich to dinner.

26

Lepers Without a Leper Mission

My grandmother was a godly woman. She was always involved in our lives, daily praying for us and loving us. In a variety of ways, she served in her local church and always had a keen interest in missions.

An early memory I have of her at home was the sight of her knitting long, narrow, white strips of material. I remember asking what they were for. She said that they were leper bandages she was knitting for a leper mission in India, which, as she explained, was far away. How interesting, I thought, that here in our city was a grandmother knitting long bandages for leopards in India. I knew that leopards were different from tigers, but I did not know that they would need bandages. Maybe they were like the lion with the thorn in his foot. I wondered where this leopard mission was.

I came to realize later that lepers were different from leopards. But I still marvel that half a world away people were making an effort to help people with a dreadful disease.

I now realize that there are some diseases of the spirit that are worse than leprosy. After all, leprosy is not something one typically gets by sinning. Separation is. Regardless of who leaves and what the ratio of my failures/your failures might be, in a separation both parties have failed. The separation was not a matter of random chance, even though the statistics say that the odds favor marriage breakdown. There was always sin. One could have been more kind, sensitive, caring. A death can be explained away by saying, "This is God's will for us," but a separation is always just a mess.

Worse yet is the label "outcast" applied to separated and divorced persons by many in religious circles. We all have lists of bad sins and worst sins. Separation is one of the worst. It is easy to see why. If the person who knew one the best, who vowed to love one unconditionally forever, for better or for worse until death, leaves, what value does one have? Anne's walking out on the marriage shouts to all that I am not worth it. People are reluctant to disagree with Anne. After all, she knew me best.

Lepers had colonies in which to live. Where do the separated go? The natural answer is to go to church. But there is a high price in going to church when you are separated. It is organized on a family and normative basis. The separated are a perceived risk to both the marrieds and the singles. No one knows what to say to them. Yet those who have been left are usually the strongest advocates of the value of marriage a church can have. We can assure people that the grass is not greener and that working out your problems is the best answer. It is hard for religious people to deal with sinners like the separated. Maybe it would be easier if they remembered that we the separated are just sinners saved by grace who are very conscious of our sinfulness. Maybe if when I was married, I had been more aware that I, too, was always just a sinner saved by grace, I might have been a better help to the separated I had known. Lepers have a mission reaching out to them. Whose task is it to reach out to me in my pain and sickness? I am a leper without a leper mission.

27

Patient Terminal—Do Not Revive

Despair is a strange experience. It is a time when your world gets smaller and smaller. Options narrow and you feel trapped. You experience a feeling of hopelessness and grief that is bigger than dreams. It wells up from deep within and encompasses your entire being.

Faced with the silence of God, you reach a point of utter darkness. What is real? What does it mean to be alive? The room is so dark, and you stop groping for the door. You ask, "Does light exist at all?" You recall the brightness and warmth of God's light. But was that real? It is so dark now —was there ever any light?

In the terror that grips me when I ask that question, I want to run. I must know. Is God there? Was He ever there? Where is He now? I have spent a lifetime knowing Him. I have known countless others who know Him. But what if He is not there? What if He never was there?

My theology screams back all of the biblical truths and constructs. Of course He is there. You have experienced His presence and His grace. But where is He now? Why is He silent? How much grief does He expect me to endure? *Where are You, God?*

I trusted in the love of my wife. I was secure in her love. Yet she has told me that she is not sure that she ever loved me. She is sure that she does not love me now. *O God, it hurts.* It hurts so much. I was sure that she loved me. Had I imagined it all? It was true love—or so I thought. But now she doesn't love me. True love is always there. It is unconditional, even when it is failed. I had prayed so much for us when we were dating. Our engagement was committed to God. Our marriage had been consecrated to God. All those people at our wedding had prayed for us. Everlasting love. This sinking feeling won't go away. If I was wrong about her, am I wrong about God too? Panic grows.

I turn to You for reassurance of love, God. Have You walked away too? Were You ever there? I don't know what is real anymore. O God, it hurts so much—help me, God. I can't take it anymore.

Then a strange logic takes over. If I am not sure God exists anymore, I should go to where God is supposed to be. If He is not there, I might as well know now rather than live in this cursed life without God. To know for sure, I must die. So I write out letters to my Anne, Jeff, and Laura. I include extra letters for the children for when they are ten, twenty, and thirty years old. This is all starting to make sense. There is some relief from this doubt in sight. My plan is a simple one. I'll go to the cabin on this winter day. I'll not light a fire—just lie down and go to sleep in this sub-zero weather. Like the elderly Eskimo walking off into the storm—I'll just go to sleep and awake with God, or find out the awful truth. Either way, it is better than living out this shell of a life with everything that meant anything already smashed beyond recognition.

A friend interrupts this plan. I still think I should sue him for damages for all of the pain and suffering I have had to endure since he intervened! It all made such good sense. But my friend did not read my self-inscribed hospital chart: "Patient terminal—do not revive."

28

The World Series—Sitting on the Bench?

One of the remarkable images in Scripture is the occasion of Moses hearing from God through the burning bush. The bush attracted Moses' attention because it was burning but was not consumed.

The separation has had many strange effects on my thinking. I find myself thinking about the bush in that story. God was using it as a means of communication to Moses. It continued to burn and burn and burn. We are not told of the condition of the bush at the end of the encounter. Did it return to its preburned state? Or did it finally burn to ashes? Not much is said about the bush. It is a small object in an important moment. It had significance because God used it for His purpose. What good purpose is God using this painful experience to accomplish? Am I a burning bush?

As human beings, we understand that we have value because we were created in God's image. Perhaps it is during those times when we see God using us to benefit others that our faith seems most alive. In spite of my theology, I have felt more spiritually energized when I have been able to give of myself to others. When in the process of serving the needs of others I have seen God bless those people, I have experienced a great sense of oneness with God. I have been a channel of God's grace.

In my situation now, I feel as though I have been benched by the manager in the World Series. You know the clichés: "There is no dress rehearsal for life"; "You only go around once"; "I shall pass this way but once." This is the big game. Our moments do count. So why am I on the bench? Is it because I blew it? Is it because the coach wants me to think about the game? Did I look tired? (No, this is definitely not a rest.) Or was I injured and am now on the disabled list? What is going on here? How is this good?

Time is ultimately the most valuable resource. Life is short. As I have watched the changes in my Jeff and Laura during this year of separation, I have had the sense of being cheated because of the limited contact imposed on me by the separation and my priority to seek reconciliation. All this time alone seems so unhealthy and wasted.

The example of Moses is helpful. He went through his own periods of activity and isolation. Is this my forty years in Midian? It seemed like such a waste of his abilities. And what of the generation who suffered under the Egyptians for an extra forty years? What followed in the wilderness must not have seemed like much of an improvement to Moses. There was the high of the escape from Egypt and the parting of the Red Sea. He had the opportunity to be with God on the mountain. But the wilderness and the murmuring people lasted a long time.

People tell me that God is using this time to mold and shape me. All good statements. They talk about Moses, Joseph, David, and other biblical characters who seemed to be benched for a while. But in this separation I wonder. If it leads to divorce, will I have an experience like one of those people from the Bible, or will I be like Cain, who was marked by God and had to experience being cursed all of his life? Am I an Ishmael who will be sent away from my people because of my new status?

I feel God's fire right now. Is it His refining fire or the fire of His judgment? Or is it just the heat of being in the kitchen of life? It would help if I could believe that I was the burning bush—it's hot, but it's OK because God is using me in this. I wish I knew.

Coach, can You tell me why I am on the bench? Will I get to play again? I want the team to win because this is important—eternal destinies are in the balance. If it is best for the team, I guess I can sit it out. Don't be mad at me, Coach. I have blown it lots of times. But I tried, Coach. I really tried. Talk to me, Coach. Help me understand. I just wish I knew.

29

Courting Disaster

The idea of taking another Christian to court is foreignto me. To think of being in court with my wife is sickening. But that is where I have been.

Shortly after Anne left, we were due for a remortgaging on our home. While Anne was across the continent visiting her parents, I had sought to renew the mortgage with the same firm. I discussed with Anne the terms and conditions of the mortgage, and she said to go ahead.

On the day that the remortgaging was due to be signed, I received a call from the mortgage company saying that they had received a call from my wife's lawyer, who wanted to review the documents before she signed. That was how I learned that Anne had retained a lawyer.

I had the unhappy experience of meeting him as I went in to sign the papers for the mortgage, since there was not time to execute the documents elsewhere. He began by saying that I should understand that he was acting on behalf of my wife in more than just this mortgage. They were concerned that I not "skip off to Brazil" with the mortgage money. I assured him that I had no travel plans and that my attention was only on how to repair the marriage. I learned later that he had been recommended to her by someone in her new church. Praise the Lord for such helpful people.

I have had very positive experiences with lawyers in business, but this kind of adversarial process produces no winners. The last thing that I wanted in our situation was a lawyer. It reminded me of that old joke, "What do you call five hundred lawyers at the bottom of the ocean? An excellent start."

Over the next couple of months I was reluctant to retain a lawyer of my own. I knew how that tends to escalate the war. So I responded to their actions and insistence on different actions by making my best judgment in a spirit of cooperation.

Once Anne quit the counseling process relating to the children, I—and others—appealed for her not to go the route of lawyers but to enter mediation, which is a more constructive process of problem solving relating to the children. Even our former pastor, Bing, was unable to reach her with those appeals. She wanted the power and security of a lawyer.

Anne then began to limit my access to the children and had begun imposing her will on them without discussion. That combined with the fact that she had dropped out of counseling forced me to begin a painful shift. My priorities had always been Anne first and the children a close second. Since I knew that a healthy marriage was in the best interests of the children, I had kept my focus on Anne and put up with the children's being in a difficult situation. It was clear to me that if I made an issue of the children, it would give her another excuse to resist any thought of reconciliation. My counselor agreed. How do I choose between my love for my wife and my love for my children? It is all so sick.

Finally, I came to the point where I had to begin to respond to the children's unmet needs in living with Anne. I sought out a family law attorney whose approach was conciliatory rather than confrontational. Yet even with warnings of the probability of a court action, Anne would not negotiate or mediate. We attempted repeated contacts and proposals with her lawyers but they would not deal. It was in their interest to maintain the status quo.

I began a court action for a joint custody order and, failing that, sole custody. In the interim between the time the papers were served and the court date, our pastor again appealed to Anne to negotiate. I made what I thought was a generous proposal to her through Bing. She listened and gave a noncommittal response. The clock was ticking, and we ended up in court.

On that day in May we were able to negotiate an agreement between the lawyers and ourselves in the lobby outside the courtroom. It provided for joint custody but limited my time to every other weekend for four days. I was able to secure four of the eight weeks with the children in the summer. I hoped that being in joint custody we would be able to work together and that it might demonstrate to her my willingness to cooperate with her. I hoped that it would minimize the tension and keep the door for reconciliation open a crack. We were to restructure the agreement in September when Jeff would start school. I could wait.

As September came and went, Anne and her lawyer refused to respond to our attempts to renegotiate. Anne's relationship with the children continued to deteriorate. She continued to appear to be avoiding her problems. The risk to the children was becoming severe. It was clear that she was unable or unwilling to work jointly in our care of the children. She labeled our son Jeff as manipulative and had increased the physical discipline of the children.

I made the decision to focus on the children's needs rather than Anne's. I changed law firms and hired the best family law attorney in our state. We would do what needed to be done to protect the children. It seems that a custody battle is inevitable. I will have to trust that the sovereignty of

God will lead to the best resolution of these problems. It has been the only way to protect the children.

In our state, the custody process will force us both to undergo three months of psychiatric evaluation to determine who would be the better parent for the children. Could it be that this intensive counseling evaluation will be a place where Anne will face her need to confront herself as she is?

I did not want this battle. She chose the legal weapons. If it was to do with anything other than the children, I would not need the legal system. But all of the professionals involved believe that her problems are real. They also believe that the best interests of the children are not being served in the status quo. I feel as though I am on a river paddling hard to go upstream but watching the current drag me toward the falls anyway. She chose to use a lawyer. She is courting disaster for all of us.

30

Love in Any Language

Anne enjoyed singing solos in churches and in other ministry settings. I always felt a special glow when it was a Sunday when I would be preaching after she sang. She was very effective. She communicated.

Remarkably, she has been soloing in churches and other settings since she left. One of the songs she has been singing is "Love in Any Language." What does she mean when she sings those words? What does love mean to her? What language of love is she hearing or speaking in her choices?

We had talked a great deal about our love for each other in the three years before we married. We had spent a year together at school. We had spent a year six hundred miles apart. Oh, the phone bills. Oh, the weekends of twenty-four hours of driving and sixteen hours of being together. I can still hear that Gordon Lightfoot extra-long tape playing over and over as I drove those long nights to and from a visit with her.

Where is the love that I thought was ours? We had talked about love's ultimately being an act of our will. It was our whole being joined as one. Two individuals complementing each other and serving each other blending into an image of Christ and the church. Ultimately, it was the same unconditional love God has for us.

Now I hear her say that she does not love me. She is not sure that she ever loved me. Anne has said that she knew the day after she was married that she had made a big mistake. The marriage was death for her. Now she has freedom. Her emotions can be expressed without my interference. She does not care what anybody else thinks or what effect this has on anyone else. She is taking care of herself. That is most important.

What do I make of all this? Did she never love me? Was I fooled by her for all those years? Was it just an act? How can I trust her about anything again? How can I trust anyone again?

Or is she looking in the rearview mirror and reinterpreting the marriage to fit her new decision? Is she stringing the tough times together and presenting that as the picture of our marriage? Am I stringing together the good times and saying that was our marriage? Am I ignoring the experiences of rejection by her? Was it as bad as she thinks, or as good as I remember? Is it the simple answer of somewhere in between?

Anne has been unwilling to meet with me to talk about repairing the marriage. We did meet one evening when she told me that she was not coming back. With all of my heart, I reviewed with her at the restaurant my failures and weaknesses. I had been thinking about those things for the month since she had left. I assured her that apart from sacrificing my personal relationship with God, I would make whatever changes were necessary to heal our marriage. I outlined changes I had already made. Whether it was a geographical move, a change in occupation, a new lifestyle—everything was on the table. She was the priority. I saw how she interpreted that meeting when we went to court five months later.

In her affidavit, she said that I had made commitments to change but that my promises were "hollow and insincere." She damned me with that sentence. She stabbed me with a knife that continues to turn in my heart.

I love her with an unconditional love. It is not a naive love that stops when she hurts, offends, or fails me. I know all too well how human we both are. But I married her for better or for worse, for richer and for poorer, in sickness and in health, till death us do part. I meant those words. I made the choice to love her forever. I thought that she did, too.

What did she mean with those words? It is as though the Anne I knew died the day she left. What if she does divorce me? What is my responsibility? I don't want to choose to stop loving her. What is right? What can I live with? *O God, it hurts.*

What view of love do her actions communicate to the children? They know that Mommy does not *like* Daddy anymore. They know that Mommy does not *love* Daddy anymore. They are worried that if Mommy could stop loving Daddy, maybe she will stop loving them, too. They test me. Do I still love Mommy? Do I still love them? Will God always love them? What can I do? *O God, it hurts.*

Did she ever love me? I am not satisfied with love in any language. I want it to be love in God's language. Anything else has too many loopholes. *O God, I miss her.*

31

Life in a Minor Key— I Hate Key Changes

It has been tough to be in the middle of such a negative experience for so long. I have a new appreciation for some of the minor key psalms, black spirituals, and country hurtin' songs. They are all full of the emotions of helplessness and hopelessness. Even in the psalms of pain, the hope often is eternal rather than in this life. Gone is my basic positive life view. My life is now in a minor key, and I hate this key change.

When I am with friends, I am conscious how negative my words have become. The separation seems to find its way into conversation no matter what the topic. It is so overwhelming. But I don't want to become one of those cynical, negative people.

It seemed that I could usually find ways to encourage others in my former life. Now it seems that the encouragement I bring to my friends is that they are not going through what I am facing.

How do I stay positive in the midst of my pain? Does God really want to take away all of my happiness? I am not as righteous as Job, so I know that it is probably not some divine contest. But even Job kept his wife during his suffering. I am all alone. Tammy Faye stayed with Jim. Why were things so bad that Anne had to leave?

Ugh. I hate being negative. Will I become like Charlie Brown—awaiting the next disaster? I wouldn't want to be around someone like me. *How much more do I have to take, God?* "A little more" is not an encouraging answer.

I am so weak, God. Even the prospect of heaven does not bring a sense of joy. My spirit is battered and torn. I used to be able to sing "If Heaven Never Was Promised to Me." I could say that the difference of Christ in my life had been significant enough that even if there were no heaven, it was worth it. My separation forces life-wrenching questions to the surface. *God, with friends like You, who needs evil? Where are You, God? Did I ever know You? Was it all in my imagination? Was Your love a phantom just like Anne's? What do I really know?*

There I go again, being negative. Life in a minor key—I hate key changes. I hope that there will be at least one more. I long to leave these death dirges and get back to a positive major key again soon.

32

Learning to Walk Again

It is such a strange feeling to be emotionally and psychologically paralyzed. It is as though I have broken my neck or back and must spend a long time in a hospital bed. Initially, I could do nothing. It was clear that it would take me a long time to learn to walk again.

My work is a form of self-employment. Many days I wished that it was sweeping floors. This job requires me to make things happen. For the better part of a week after Anne left I could do nothing at all. I could not even make the phone calls to cancel my schedule. Fortunately, I had an associate, Jerry, who was there to run interference for me as I sat in shock.

My energy level went from an sixteen-hour day to nothing. It was frustrating, but there was nothing I could do about it. After a few weeks, I was able to progress to special events or speaking engagements. I dreaded the moments up to when they began. Then I had the energy for the time needed. Moments afterwards, I collapsed and needed to go home. What a basket case!

Somehow, when the children were with me, I could rise to the challenge—even for a week. Perhaps it was the sense that their need was greater than my need. Perhaps it was just God's grace for them.

So many days it has been like lying face down in three inches of water. It was as though I were drowning but could not find the energy to turn over or stand up. I was helpless.

As the first months have passed, I can sense some improvement. I am able to do more for longer periods of time. I am taking those first tentative steps again. Oh, I feel so weak. My balance is so uncertain.

As much as things are better, I am still subject to setbacks. A tough word from a friend, financial pressure, and especially any negatives from Anne can set me back weeks. I have had to learn that my recovery is a zigzag and not a straight line. It has been tough to get used to that sense of vulnerability. It is hard to feel certain. It is hard to feel safe.

I remind myself to beware of the Lilliputians. In *Gulliver's Travels,* Gulliver is held captive by the little people of Lilliput, who use tiny ropes to hold down the sleeping giant. I must watch for a series of little stresses that can combine to pin me down. Being around critical or uncaring people is a sure way to become trapped. Sometimes I have to take the tougher initial action of saying no to negative encounters rather than trying to cope with their aftermath.

I worry that people will think that I am like the comedy character in the TV series "SCTV, Guy Caballero." When Joe Flarehty played the title character, a station manager, he drove around in a wheelchair. Everyone knew that he could walk. He would walk in some scenes, but he was normally in that chair.

I hope that I know when it is time to get up and walk without my crutches or wheelchair. Many people tell me how well I am doing. I have to remind them that I'm not doing well. I am an emotional wreck. I am still crawling, not running a one-hundred-yard dash.

But I am learning to walk again—one painful step at a time.

33

It Was the Worst of Times, It Was the Worst of Times

Dickens's *Tale of Two Cities* begins with the statement "It was the best of times. It was the worst of times." My tale of this separation is that "It was the worst of times. It was the worst of times."

My inner world and my outer world were both in shambles. In one fateful decision by Anne, I had been destroyed. The old Pat had been killed just as quickly as by an assassin.

I had been Anne's husband, lover, friend, partner, and soul mate. Now I was her mistake.

Our ministries together—past, present, and future—were unalterably changed. The little church begun a year earlier with two other families had started with Anne's enthusiasm but died within a couple of weeks of the separation. Our group of thirty-five nonbelievers had many who I believe were close to salvation. They were cut adrift—too few believers to form a nucleus for others to continue. My roles in the denomination ended with my resignations. I wanted there to be no doubt to Anne that my priorities had been and always were my personal relationship with God, my family, my ministries, and then my jobs. She said that she knew that and that it was not a lack of time with her and the kids. If she divorced, I could anticipate no ministry opportunities in our denomination.

I lost all of the opportunities for fellowship and growth that those experiences provided. I faced a huge vacuum. There was no church to retreat into for healing. I was all alone.

My business depended on my ability to communicate effectively and confidently. How could I appear confident when my whole being had been ripped away? I couldn't, and the business floundered in what were already tough times in a deep recession.

Our new home, which could have been the place we lived from then to retirement, was forced to be sold by Anne. She had moved north with the children. To be near them, I moved into that community as well. I felt like a P.O.W. I was behind enemy lines in her world. There were no support systems in this town for me. I was the outcast. She was the one in control.

To finish me off, she decided to publicize with friends and others my many weaknesses and failures. The dark side of all intimate relationships, where we are transparent, is one of the first weapons used by a vindictive spouse.

It was the worst of times. It was the worst of times.

34

Life as a Jukebox—Stuck on B-17

It used to be that when I heard sad songs on the radio, I thought of teenagers who had fallen out of love. It never occurred to me that the songs probably were about lost spouses and broken marriages. Now I know why Olivia Newton-John asks the man not to play B-17. I am stuck on B-17.

It seems that the radio is haunted. Christian or secular artists all cause me pain because of my association of that music with Anne. I was never a big fan of country music. It always seemed too cloying and artificial with all of the hurtin' songs. More often than not, they are songs of the separated. They are almost always written by the "Left." They are songs of pining and despair. But the songs are honest in their pain. I hear the words on many old songs with new ears. There is much pain out there.

There are so many things in our world to stab the separated. It can be a sermon illustration on families. It can be a TV commercial picturing a couple walking hand in hand. Anything that shows what life used to be like savages me. Even when I drive by some children in a day-care I am reminded that I cannot go today to see my children because they are with Anne. *O God, it hurts.*

I pass the apartment building where Anne was living when I proposed to her. I go by the exit for the road where we used to live a few months ago. All around me are memories of what was.

Our lives were integrated. Food. Music. Sports. Travel. They all have some memory of her. How do I rebuild a life when everything prompts a memory of her? I wonder if any of the inhabitants of medieval monasteries were trying to forget? But I know that the silence is no friend, either.

When I take the children to a restaurant the waitress asks whether I want to wait until my wife arrives before ordering. I often answer that the restaurant will be closed before she arrives, and none of us can wait that long. It is tempting to answer that my wife died. Given the changes in Anne, it seems that the wife I knew died on that cold night when she drove away.

The pain is all around me. Waves of nostalgia, memories, and despair can be triggered without warning. There is no defense against it. I just must tell people that I'm sorry, but I am stuck on B-17.

35

On the Yellow Brick Road

One of my favorite childhood stories was the *Wizard of Oz*. It was such a rich tale of imagination. In it were good and evil, hope and despair, friend and foe.

I have often thought of the song sung by Judy Garland, "Somewhere over the Rainbow." In the middle of my tornado it is pleasant to think of a place where happy little bluebirds fly.

It is curious that Dorothy never received much real help or advice from the characters in her story. Some were there at critical moments, and being together brought encouragement, but more often than not Dorothy was left to make her own choices.

She was told that she should head to the Emerald City to see the Wizard Of Oz. She also learned that she should "Follow the Yellow Brick Road." But apart from that, she was given precious little guidance for the journey.

In one scene, she comes to a fork in the Yellow Brick Road. She asks aloud which way she should go. To her amazement, a scarecrow speaks. "Some people go this way.

Some people go that way. And some people go both ways!" Ultimately, she chose one of the forks for no particular reason.

The Bible seems to focus more on who we are to be and how we are to be rather than on which choices we should make when there is no obvious answer. At so many tough points in this separation journey, I have been faced with crucial decisions for which there were no clear answers. There are no handbooks written for this set of circumstances. If a book were to be written about it, it would be so unbelievable it would be placed in the fiction section.

There have been very few points where others could really give me clear advice. As with most of life, the tough choices have been mine to make. But it has been especially difficult, because I no longer trust my judgment. After all, if my past decisions have got me into this mess, how can my future choices not make it worse?

Friends have helped to clarify my thinking and check my attitudes. But at most of the forks in the road, I have had to make a gut decision and trust that God's sovereignty would overrule.

It has been helpful in making those choices to face as honestly as I could my memories of life with Anne. With a decade of marriage and three years of dating, there were many from which to choose. Six months into the separation, I made a trip back to my alma mater. I walked around the campus. So many places Anne and I were in those happy days seemed to mourn with me. So much had changed. But I felt safe. It still felt OK. Those had been good times. The campus was still real. Life could go on. Life as a student seemed far away. But there was comfort in even that long ago.

I have gone on some nostalgia drives. They have taken me by old places we used to live and play in. Dad always used to say, "Face your fears." I had to confront the ghosts and let them stab me. Then they would not have the same power over my future.

Like Dorothy, I am afraid that if I do reach Oz and meet the Wizard, there will be nothing in his bag for me, either. There certainly is a shortage of magic wands. I must walk on this journey and face my enemies of doubt and fear. Others may travel with me, but no one else can show me the way back to my Kansas.

I want to go home. I miss her so much. Maybe if I click my heels together three times . . .

36

Out to Pasture with Nebuchadnezzar

When Nebuchadnezzar fell under God's judgment, he went insane for seven years. Insanity drove him out to pasture to eat grass. What a strange sight to the people of his nation to see their former king out acting like an animal.

I struggle with whether I am under God's judgment or whether my fate is part of living in a sin-sick world. What I do know is that, like Nebuchadnezzar, I am out to pasture. And the grass doesn't taste very good! I don't know how conscious the king was of his actions or the people around him. I know that I am painfully aware of a great sense of failure and despair.

There are times when I feel that, even when I am alone, I am in bad company. The separation is a form of insanity. What do my friends think as they look at me? What about the people we had served in ministry? Do they gloat? Does it shake their faith? *O God, this damages so many people. Why won't You stop it?* Like the deadly cloud following a nuclear blast, the death drifts in so many directions. So many people beyond those close to the explosion are affected.

It is as though I have been buried alive—above ground. I can see Anne. I can see the people around me. But I cannot breathe. *Won't somebody help me? I'm dying, God. I'm losing my mind.* This has been the year of the living dead. I feel like a wraith.

Everything is out of control. I am on the end of Anne's yo-yo. She is pulling and pushing when it suits her. She can let out more string or pull me in at will. I just keep spinning. *O Lord, how long does this have to last? When will You rescue us from this misery?* Does she realize what she is doing?

What would it be like to be hospitalized? How can I keep from cracking? The pressure is intense, and it is going on and on. I can hang on if I know it will have a happy ending, but I know that divorce is an incurable disease. Will people understand if I do crack? I've got to hang on for the kids. What if all of these character-building experiences are to prepare me for something worse?

Oh, well. Spring will be here soon. Maybe I can find some nice spring grass. Then I can be out to pasture with Nebuchadnezzar.

37

A Friend in Need— Has Few Friends in Deed

We're steering clear from you for the next while until things get cleared up. It's nothing personal. You know that it is nothing personal." This from a couple of my closest friends who did not want to be caught in the middle of our war. They had been out of touch for a few months since the separation in spite of my efforts to reach out to them. I finally received some honesty from them. What is left of a friendship like that after a war is over? Not much. What was there before the separation? I don't know. People have such different reactions to the separated.

Some of the reactions probably are a statement of what the relationship really was. Other responses may be a way of coping with their confusion or disappointment in seeing friends split up. Who wants to choose sides?

Initially, I did not want people to choose sides. Anne made up a list of my friends/your friends. Some declared themselves early to be supporting her. Some tried to keep up contact with both. Others tried to reach out to her and were rebuffed because they did not support her decision. They stopped reaching out and were written off by Anne as victims of Pat's manipulation.

As time has passed, I have struggled with the three or four people who have tried to stay in touch with both of us. This is is especially true of those who have said things such as "I keep Anne's confidences, and I keep yours." I am not sure I want someone with two mental drawers marked Morgan—one for Anne and one for Pat. More than loyalty to me as a friend (which I do want), I want someone who is loyal to the idea of "married for life." Especially during this phase of the separation, when all things are possible, I am troubled by people who respond that she has made up her mind and that is it.

One of my friends reflected how when he has been off the path, he has been grateful that God has not taken the proverbial two-by-four to him to get his attention. I responded by saying that if I am doing as much damage to as many people as Anne is by her choice, I hope that God would take a two-by-four to me. (Having said that, I wonder if this separation is the two-by-four. Ugh.)

It is tough to maintain the status quo in our relationships at any time in life—they are always changing. When there has been a breach like this, it seems friends have to choose which side of the crevice they will stand on. Anne has said that most of our old friends have stayed with me. It would come as a surprise to her how few have stayed with either of us.

One of the most useful roles that friends have played is to talk about our past. When they reflect ways that Anne and I positively influenced their lives, or life in general, it really helps. During a time when you doubt every aspect of who you are and who you were, those reference points are encouraging. At that point in time, it was good. I do not have to buy into Anne's reinterpretation that it was all bad. My life did have meaning. We did make a contribution to someone else. Maybe there will be a future when I can benefit others again.

Two of my friends upon hearing of Anne's separation came to visit. Both were friends from college days. Each traveled at different times across the continent to spend some time with me. In those early days, those and other emotional paramedics helped me survive. As we sat in my half-empty house, they grieved with me. There were no easy answers. But by being physically present, Charles and Jared gave me hope.

It is shocking how few friends any of us really have. Anne and I have nurtured many relationships over many years, but most have evaporated. That refining process has helped me value the golden friendships that are there.

Acts of kindness have shouted hope to me in my silence. All of the prayers, phone calls, cups of coffee, dinners, cards, letters, notes, tapes, and visits have said to me that there can be life after Anne. And that is the awful question that the separated must face every day. Those friends in deed have been a crucial part of this friend in need's survival. I thank God for them.

38

Ravens in the Backyard

In the Old Testament, there are many illustrations of God's care for His people. Although there was general protection of them, during a crisis or great need His servants or the nation became more aware of His faithfulness to them. Those accounts are potent reminders for people who are struggling. But like Israel's, our memory is short and our faith is small when we are tested. I am reminded of ravens.

Elijah had just faced down the faithless King Ahab and had announced God's judgment on the land. A terrible drought was to begin to bring repentance. The problem with judgments is that they usually affect many lives beyond the ones who have made the choice to rebel against God. But in spite of the hardship that came, the heavenly Father showed mercy to His servant Elijah. The prophet was sent to the brook of Kerith. By faith, Elijah went.

There God provided him water to drink from the brook while the drought spread and devastated the land. God sent a raven with food for Elijah. Those were still tough times for the prophet, who did not have the freedom of movement and variety of food he had enjoyed before. He was imprisoned by the circumstances created by the king's rebellion. It was very unfair. But God sustained His servant through the crisis. There is no record that Elijah benefited beyond his needs for that day. But those needs were met.

My financial circumstances have gone from a platinum credit rating to the edge of fiscal oblivion. The economy, the emotional collapse of the separation, the legal fees, and the custody battle zapped me. My income, which had fluctuated in the six-figures while I was in business, now had five-figure losses. I was approaching the GDP of some third world countries. The decline was steeper than any roller coaster ride at Great America.

Try as I did, it was impossible to make money. My business required confidence and sparkle. Now I was only confident that my sparkle had gone. I had gone as a person from a growth stock to a penny stock. (And the shares were all on margin with the loan about to be called.)

As I would cry out to God about this additional pressure I would ask, Why this too? Why did I have to face bankruptcy as well as separation? Those were Anne's choices, not mine. Why can't I prosper at least in this area when everything else has been taken away from me? Like a wet towel, everything in my being was being twisted and squeezed. Couldn't there be a little light somewhere?

As much as we would pray or wish for God to intervene in a crisis by taking us out of it, sometimes His answer is to help us survive it. I prefer deliverance, but as God has chosen to respect our free will, that sometimes means that the choices of another person change my life. Why does one sick person get better and another die? That and many other questions like it do not have answers that make sense to us. It may be comforting to postpone such questions to eternity, but I am not sure that an answer different from "sin" will be given there, either. We live in a broken world of broken people marred by sin. God's love has always been in spite of sin.

Until the "age which is to come" completely replaces this "present evil age" there will be many choices and relationships in need of redemption.

Like Elijah, I would relearn that God cares for me a day at a time in all areas of my life. Regardless of the size of my bank account, it is always just a day at a time.

There have been days when I have not had a dollar to my name. In town, I have been panhandled by one of the locals on those dollarless days. I asked him if he was broke. He said yes. I replied that I would be very happy to be just broke. It would take me tens of thousands of dollars to just get back to broke.

I am not sure that this comparison encouraged him at all. Yet a year later, there is still food to eat, clothes to wear, a roof over my head, and a car to drive. It is a long way from where I was. It is very much like my first year out of college as an assistant pastor.

In the darkest times of financial need, my faith allowed that God would send the ravens to sustain me during this drought. I could imagine our old backyard filled with a month's supply of ravens all waiting for me there. I do hope that they received the change of address notice.

At the outset of the separation, I sat in tears and yielded everything to God anew. Like Frodo Baggins at the gates of Moria, I said that I do not want to go but I will go though I do not know the way. I went through a long list of what was my life and gave it all back to God. Whatever it takes for me to be what You want me to be, I will by faith yield. Marriage, custody, health, ministry, reputation, home, money—all were forfeit. The sifting began and continues to this day. All of the above except my health have been lost. But I have gained a faith I could never have known at all if those good things had remained. I recommend the outcome, but I would not recommend the route.

God has sent the ravens to me. I have had just what I needed at that time and usually only at the last moment.

Those ravens have taken the shape of family, friends, church, denomination, and even an IRS refund (God does have a sense of humor). Almost always it was help unlooked for and given sacrificially beyond their resources. I am still not comfortable receiving—it is easier to give than to receive. But I am learning. Excuse me, I see a raven coming.

39

My Love, My Enemy

My love, my enemy. How can both statements be so true of one person at the same time? Only in this contradiction called a marital separation can it be so.

No one has loved me more deeply. No one has wounded me so severely. No one has brought me greater joy. No one has brought me greater sadness. I had known her unconditional acceptance. I now know her uncompromising rejection.

My loving partner who with me created two wonderful children is now my adversary in their custody. So much pain. So many who suffer. No winners. Only losers.

It is as though I am being carried along by a great wind against which I have no strength. I don't want to see her hurt. Does she know what she is doing to me? Does she know what price our children are paying and will pay for the rest of their lives? How can one who was so good become so bad?

I miss my love. I don't know who this person is. She looks like Anne. But she is not the Anne I knew.

I have heard how tough it is for a police officer or soldier to shoot an enemy dressed in his own uniform. He can't shoot one of his own.

Anne likes to talk about how the church has failed her since the separation. She describes herself in the imagery of the song "Wounded Soldier." That song appeals to God not to let another wounded soldier die. To me, it seems as though my Anne has shot others and herself and is now complaining that fellow believers are not reaching out to her. She does not seem to realize that she continues to fire her gun at all who approach. She seems unable to see that her choice to separate is a great wound inflicted on me and others. Certainly she has been wounded by me, by people we have served in ministry settings, and by life in general. But her choice to separate will only make her wounds fester more.

I must leave Anne's fate in God's hands. I will not act against her regarding our marriage. He has a much greater love for her and a deeper commitment than any human could have—even a husband. *O God, I want to trust You to help her. But it has been so long. There has been no improvement. It all seems so hopeless.*

But what can I do about Jeff and Laura? I must protect them. Do I now have to see my love as my enemy in this? I can't let them continue to suffer. Anne seems unable to see what their needs really are or the effect that her problems are having on them. *O God, how do I choose between my wife and my children?*

It is all so wrong. But I am helpless to change it. All of the time I have given to allow for healing has just been time for the rupture to grow. Now there is a great gulf fixed between us. We need a bridge. So many key people have worked against us to support her decision to leave. So many others have reached out to her to heal this breach. All efforts have failed. My love. My enemy. God alone can help us now.

40

A Prayer of Faith for the Separated

And we know that in all things God works for the good of those who love him, who have been called according to his purpose. For those God foreknew he also predestined to be conformed to be the likeness of his Son, that he might be the firstborn among many brothers. And those he predestined, he also called; those he called, he also justified; those he justified, he also glorified.

"What, then, shall we say in response to this? If God is for us, who can be against us? He who did not spare His own Son, but gave him up for us all—how will he not also, along with him, graciously give us all things? Who will bring any charge against those whom God has chosen? It is God who justifies. Who is he that condemns? Christ Jesus, who died—more than that, who was raised to life—is at the right hand of God and is also interceding for us. Who shall separate us from the love of Christ? Shall trouble or hardship or persecution or famine or nakedness or danger or sword? As it is written:

'For your sake we face death all day long;
we are considered as sheep to be slaughtered.'

No, in all these things we are more than conquerors through him who loved us. For I am convinced that neither death nor life, neither angels nor demons, neither the present nor the future, nor any powers, neither height nor depth, nor anything else in all creation, will be able to separate us from the love of God that is in Christ Jesus our Lord."

Romans 8:28-38

Lord, I believe. Help my unbelief. Amen.

Epilogue

This book was written during my separation period asan exercise to explore the feelings, contradictions, and confusion of that time. I hoped that it would also serve as a way of sharing with our children when they are grown what it was like for me.

Anne chose to divorce me shortly after our year of separation was complete.

The months since the divorce have been filled with new and different experiences as I learn not just about separation but also about divorce. As I reviewed this collection of experiences from my separation, there were many aspects of it that I would change. This is not a book about where I am today, but I think it accurately relates where I was during the separation. It is tempting to rewrite it with the benefit of hindsight, but that would radically change its nature. We do not stand still as we continue the process called life. This book is a record of what it was like for me to be in the hurricane. I now can look at the damage done and begin the long clean-up process. But that is another book.

Obviously, this book is not the "whole story" of our relationship or of the separation period. Almost a decade of marriage and very diverse experiences would fill many books. Nor is this a book in which you will learn all there is to know about me, my wife, or our marriage. I have chosen to disclose only some of those feelings and experiences as seen through the separation. The focus is descriptive, not prescriptive. Obviously, it is written from my perspective.

The suggestion has been made that it would be helpful to recount some of the "whys" of our marriage's failure. Some might take comfort that because our set of circumstances and choices were different from their own a breakup could not happen to them. Let me stress that we were not on anyone's list of "ten couples most likely to divorce." We had the heritage of a rich Christian experience. I am convinced that no one is immune. That may not be a comforting thought, but it should lead each couple to value the relationship they have and not take anything for granted. Ultimately, although it takes two to be married, it need only take one to divorce.

I can review the past with the benefit of the perspective of two years since the separation began. Even at this distance, I cannot give a definitive answer to the question, "Why did your marriage fail?" I can assure you that that is not the result of a lack of reflection or probing.

It is easy to look back with the benefit of hindsight and identify symptoms of problems. I can take some guesses about potential root causes, but it is impossible for me to be definitive. In the end, it boils down to the fact that Anne did not want to continue the marriage. I am convinced that, as our counselor said early on in the separation, "There is nothing here that cannot be fixed." That was not some statement of the miraculous, where all things can be repaired. It was made from the perspective of having heard each of us describe the issues important to us. But the fact was that Anne did not want to fix the marriage.

Why did she believe that the marriage was not worth any more effort? Why did she believe our marriage was beyond hope? I do not know. We have never had a conversation in which she has told me. I can certainly see many things I would do differently. I can see little moments and big ones in our marriage that I would gladly retrieve. I wish that I could package it into a neat equation identifying that this need plus that need combined with our genetics divided by our environment equals a separation. Perhaps some marriages can be diagnosed. I have not seen many that can be.

Our history included the opportunity I had shortly after she left to meet with her once again to ask for and to receive her forgiveness for my failures, insensitivity, and selfishness toward her. I had kept short accounts with her, but that final restatement was liberating for me in dealing with the past.

Although I sensed tension before the separation, I had no inkling that she was going to leave. If someone had said to me even the night before that she was going to go, it would have been news to me. We had experienced ups and downs along the way, as do many other couples, and with a tough time in business, there were lots of stress points. But we had endured and grown through those before. They certainly were not directed at Anne personally. But something did snap, and once broken it was beyond my ability to fix. I could speculate about the past and the future, but it would only be that—speculation.

I have had to relearn how little any of us has true control in life. We are all vulnerable to the choices of others and to circumstances. My experience has been a painful reminder of how careful we must be in the big and little choices we make since they can affect so many others for good or for ill.

My separation experience has been a refining process. It has melted away many nonessentials accumulated over half a lifetime. It has forced me to challenge my basic understanding of who I am and what I believe. That refining process is a typical, if painful, common denominator of all suffering. It is difficult to get worked up about traffic jams and cars that break down when one's whole life falls apart. Suffering gives one a new sense of what is really important.

Marriage, like anything in this life, is ultimately a risk. There are no guarantees of long and happy marriages. We live in an age that seeks miracles. In my third year of marriage, I preached a sermon in which I said that if we wanted to see a miracle, we should look to those believers who have been in love and married for fifty years. In our society, that constitutes a miracle. I expected to enjoy one of those miracles, too. Little did I realize how the world would look for me seven years later. Sadly, we must return to the principal message of Christianity: there is only One whose love endures forever and will not let us go.

I am thankful that I did not face this valley in my life alone. The presence of God and His grace and the help given me by people He sent to stand with me in my pain got me through even the unhappy ending I now write. God continues to work with me and on me. I am slowly being molded and shaped into what He wants me to be. It will take my whole life to get where I need to be. Ultimately, I will only catch up on the remaining rough spots at the end when Christ takes me home to heaven and I am changed. I look forward to heaven where God will wipe away my tears.

If you are interested in more information
about how to integrate principles from the Bible
with the subject matter of this book, please write
to the following address:

Northfield Publishing
215 West Locust Street
Chicago, IL 60610

My Love My Enemy

MY LOVE MY ENEMY

MEDITATIONS FOR THE SEPARATED

PAT MORGAN

NORTHFIELD PUBLISHING
CHICAGO

Northfield Publishing
A Division of MBI
Chicago, IL

ISBN: 1-881273-03-2

1 3 5 7 9 10 8 6 4 2

Printed in the United States of America